SPIRITUAL WARFARE

My Battle with Good and Evil

How to Speak Life into your Impossibilities

Frances W. Cox

Kingdom Builders Publications LLC

© 2018 Frances W. Cox
Kingdom Builders Publications, LLC

All rights reserved. No part of this book may be reproduced or transmitted in any form or by any means without written permission from the author.

Printed in the USA

ISBN 978-0-692-08448-9

Library of Congress Control Number 2018936857

Authored and illustrated by
Frances W. Cox

Editor
Kingdom Builders Publications
Wanda Brown

Photographer
Crystal Cox

Cover Design
LoMar Designs

SPIRITUAL WARFARE

CONTENTS

	ACKNOWLEDGMENT	vi
	PREFACE	vii
1	THE SEARCH FOR SPIRITUAL WARFARE	10
2	THE STRUGGLE TO PREACH IS THE CALL OF SPIRITUAL WARFARE	34
3	RECEIVING THE KEY TO SPIRITUAL WARFARE	44
4	THE WORKS AND TOOLS OF THE HOLY SPIRIT IN SPIRITUAL WARFARE	50
5	HOW TO RELEASE THE POWER OF SPIRITUAL WARFARE	76
6	THE SHEKINAH GLORY EXPERIENCE	91
7	OTHER FORMS OF SPIRITUAL WARFARE	99
	APPENDIX	111
	ABOUT THE AUTHOR	114

Frances W. Cox

ACKNOWLEDGMENTS

This book is written in memory of my parents, Ernest and Celeste Williams who were devout Christians. They were praying parents who loved the Lord and taught me and my three siblings how to pray and worship God. The greatest gift of knowing the Holy Spirit is attributed to my mother who lived to be 72 years old, while the gifts of patience, endurance and strength are attributed to my father who lived to be 94 years old.

Neither spiritual warfare nor the works of the Holy Spirit were discussed openly in those days. My mother introduced them to me at an early age through faith, prayer, and obedience. She gave me spiritual nuggets that were manifested through dreams and open visions that increased as I grew older. Her messages were powerful and spiritual. She warned me about demonic spirits and the evil forces that would come against me. Therefore, she taught me how to rise above the conflicts that I encountered in life.

My father took over this role when my mother died. I gained strength and wisdom from the many talks about the journey through life. He was full of wisdom and encouraged me to follow my own intuitions and to place my trust in God and not man. When confronted with a problem, he always answered us by saying, "Well, have you prayed about it?"

They were common everyday parents who taught us how love triumphs hatred. They showed us the true meaning of heaping coals of fire upon the heads of our enemies. More importantly, they showed us how faith and prayer are used on the battlefield of the mind to conquer spiritual battles between good and evil. Therefore, this book is dedicated to their memory and the unconditional love they showered upon me and my siblings.

PREFACE

This book is written at a time when the truth is buried beneath lies and corruption, the life of Jesus is called a fairy tale and Christianity has taken a back seat to falsehoods and political correctness. The structures and leadership of churches have changed dramatically from the inside to the outside. The steeples and crosses seen from afar were edifices to recognize the gospel church, but now there are storefront churches on every street corner and road throughout the country. The rise of these churches shows an increasing divide in doctrines and religious beliefs.

The establishment of a greater number of churches has not changed society nor the attitude or love for all people. Many of them are full of conceit, envy, hatred, and retaliation. They fail to see the guiding and evil forces in the world that are pulling the strings and manipulating their course of actions. They are in a world of denial and refuse to believe they are being manipulated by external forces drawn by a single operative, (Satan). Satan has an agenda for mankind; to control the world markets, religious leaders, food banks, morality and any foundation established by God. He uses leaders who are controlling, self-centered, and possess a narcissistic complex to do his work. Jesus warned believers in the Old Testament by revealing His spirit and appearing to them in angelic forms, visions, and dreams. He also left His Spirit to teach us through Spiritual warfare, so we can fight the good fight between good and evil through faith and prayer.

Prayer is powerful. When we put faith and prayer together along with the principles of spiritual warfare, we become mountain movers. We believe that no one has any power other than what God allows him/her to decree, declare, to speak life into impossibilities and to call things that are not, into existence. This book is written for those who know the Son, and their real purpose on earth, and to those who are searching for life and a place in the Son. This book holds the answer to the key question, what moves a living God?

THE SEARCH FOR SPIRITUAL WARFARE
Chapter 1

I searched the Scriptures for several years, looking for ways that will move God to come quickly and relieve sickness, persecution, and pain. The beginning of this search came because of the death of my brother when I was fourteen years of age. The intensity has grown in the past four years because of the war that was raging on the battlefield of my mind. I was coping with a major stroke that left me unable to walk, talk, feed or bathe myself. I was at the mercy of my youngest daughter who was living with me.

I was told that because I had missed the window where the stroke could be reversed, I would remain in this state for the rest of my life. I lost my church, my joy and my desire to be with others. I had to move from my home into a house with carpet on the floors, so I would not slip and fall when I began to walk. Not only was I a prisoner in that house, but my spirit was a prisoner locked up inside my body; a body that could not move on its own. I longed to be free. I stayed in the hospital for seven months. I was sent home and had a second major stroke on the left side of my body. I was a total wreck. Satan's attacks on my body played on my mind and caused me to forget my spiritual training. Many memories of the past raced through my mind.

I began to grieve the death of my husband and father that occurred nine years ago. I buried myself in my work during that time and did not have time to grieve their death. Now I had nothing but time, and every past thought and deed entered my head. My head felt like a trash compactor. I found myself asking

SPIRITUAL WARFARE

God to forgive me for every thought that was not about Him. I had faith that I would overcome my illness, but my body was not hearing my thoughts. I began to speak healing over my body and have my daughters play spirit-filled music and read healing Scriptures, but things were not working fast enough. I knew I had to find a way to really reconnect with God and rekindle the fire I once felt while in His presence. Since I had a lot of time on my hand and was not going anywhere, I set out again, searching for His Spirit, the same Spirit that guided me throughout my life. The spirit of infirmity had caused me to take my focus off God and replaced it with paralysis and dullness of my mind. I had to overcome this state of mind, so, I focused on the Holy Spirit. I played Whitney Houston's song, "I Love the Lord," morning, noon and night. I played it four times in the morning, four times in the evening and four times at night. I played it once for the Father, once for the Son, once for the Holy Spirit and once for the Devil, because I wanted him to know who I belong to. I belong to God. Therefore, I had to show Satan by engaging in warfare with him.

When I think about the beginning of spiritual warfare, I am taken back to the death of my brother. Willie B. and I grew up together, along with three other siblings. We were in church every time the doors opened. My parents raised us to trust and believe in God for all things. However, when Willie got sick with cancer of the blood my whole world crumbled. I recall making a pact with God during my youth for the life of my brother. When doctors gave up on him, he was sent home. I recalled the day when his cancer was diagnosed incurable, he and his wife came home to live with us. She was two months pregnant at the time but only stayed with us for a month. She could not stomach the sight of blood coming from Willie's body. Therefore, my mother would bathe, wash his sheets and keep his body and clothes clean.

Willie wanted my mother, and no one else to read to him from the Bible. When she finished washing and feeding him, she got the Bible and began reading the words of God. I knew my mother was hurting on the inside, but she never showed it on the outside. She read verses **John 14** which says, *"Let not your heart be troubled; you believe in God, believe also in me. In my Father's house are many mansions; if it were not so, I would have told you. I go to prepare a place for you. And if I go and prepare a place for you, I will come again and receive you to myself; that where I am, there you may be also."* ***(KJV)***

Willie B. asked questions while my mother read to him. She politely paused and answered them all. After several days of reading, he made his confessions openly before God and said he was ready to die. He assured momma that he no longer feared death or the unknown. I remember the loving and peaceful smile my mother wore on her face throughout that day.

She told me to give Willie to God and that one day God would give him back to us. I did not want to wait for one day. I wanted him then and longed to hear his voice. I recall the pain that filled my whole body. It was as if an elephant had sat on my chest. I could not breathe. The pain hit my heart like a giant hammer. I thought that I would surely die. I wanted to be brave for momma and daddy, but the pain and hurt were unbearable. I ran into the yard and sat under an old dogwood tree my mother and I planted from a young seedling. I cried for a long time until my eyes were red and swollen.

Figure 1

SPIRITUAL WARFARE

I decided to make a pact with God while I sat under that tree. I wanted my brother healed and alive. I wanted him alive at all cost. Although I never heard Him answer me, I told Him the conditions of the agreement. I said, "Lord if you will spare my brother's life and let him live, I promise to serve you, to go anywhere and do whatever you want me to do." I did not wait for a reply because I knew He would answer me. I was already serving Him and living a sacrificial life before Him because I loved Him and was afraid to do anything wrong.

Several days later, my brother grew worse. My father picked him up, placed him in the car and drove him to the hospital. Even then, I believed that God would heal him. My brother went into a deep coma. We all went to the hospital and sat in his room. I had no fear because I had made a pact with God and I knew He would not fail me. My mother grew tired and we came home with her, but my father went back to the hospital to stay with my brother through the night.

We were at home when I heard my mother scream. I ran down the hall into the kitchen and there she was bent over groping her chest and stomach. I asked her, "Momma, what is it?" She looked up and said, "My boy is gone." She quickly got up. I tried to console her and wanted her to console me, but she dried her tears and walked into her bedroom. I heard her praying and thanking God. I did not understand why she was thanking God for taking away her only son.

Tears began to form in my eyes. All I could think about was, "But, God, you promised me." I ran outside under that old dogwood tree and cried like a baby. I told God exactly how I felt. I was furious, angry, filled with rage and felt betrayed. I said to God, "No more, no more will I trust or believe in you again. You promised me that you would spare my brother and heal him from cancer, but, you let him die." Daddy came home. He and momma consoled each other. We all joined in a circle and held each other.

A few hours later they started preparing for the funeral and burial which were held at the family church a few miles from our home. When the burial was over, we came home. I went to that dogwood tree again to tell God that my brother would remain alive through me, but, before I could get close to the tree, a swarm of bees came over the house and from behind the tree and ran me away. I was afraid to go near that tree again. Later, that year, the tree died. I became bitter and angry because it had become a hiding place for me where I could escape from reality. I never allowed myself to trust or believe in God again. I was going through the motion of living, going to church and school just to please momma and daddy.

Figure 2

It was several years later when I realized why God allowed that tree to die. It was His way of showing me that He has power over life and death. He was letting me know that there was no help in the tree. He was showing me that He was my hiding place. I had to hide in Him. It was His way of saying, "Come let me teach you all things, old and new." This was a hard and difficult lesson to grasp at first, but once the Holy Spirit began to speak to me, revealing hidden and unknown mysteries, I understood and became a willing servant.

Many devout followers of faith have no doubt, experienced similar life-changing events that challenged their faith and caused them to question God. They had no problems, at first, believing in the power of prayer because they experienced open visions and dreams that supported their beliefs. However, when something traumatic happens to them, the struggle to regain their faith is often difficult to achieve. They want to receive faith, but they can never get beyond the earthly veil that blinds their view and distorts their belief. The veil is a combination of traditions mixed with fear, instability and false doctrines. False doctrines are manifested through the belief that Satan has all power over the earth and has a driving force which overwhelms the faith and beliefs of mankind. The Christian view that is hard to overcome is the leap of faith.

So often we are asked to believe in something we have never seen or experienced, such as the child we believed my brother would leave in his memory, but that child never saw the light of day. I thought my mother would be bitter, but she continued to smile. She shared her love between my siblings and one granddaughter, Elizabeth, six years old, who was raised in the home. Then, five years later, my oldest sister married and gave birth to our mother's first grandson. She adored him. My brother's wife never contacted us again. My mother passed away 17 years later, not ever seeing or knowing what happened to my brother's wife or the child she was supposed to be pregnant with.

When the average person believes in something or someone, and that something disappoints them, they find themselves putting up a wall. Most often, it will take another traumatic experience to contradict the first one, for them to regain their faith. of

Hebrews 11: 1 (KJV) - *Faith is the substance of things hoped for and the evidence of things not seen.*
The true leap of faith requires a person to look beyond things that exist, into a realm where nothing exists in the natural, but only in the spiritual form. Once a person gets beyond the level of sight comprehension, and into a level of spiritual comprehension, he or she can speak things into existence, just like Jesus did. When we create things in the mind, the Holy Spirit will bring those things into natural existence. I had to learn this as I was wrestling with my brother's death and the fact that his wife had cheated us of his legacy. My faith in God was tested and stretched to the limit. I began to doubt that God ever existed or that Jesus was who He said He was.

I went for months without praying or opening my Bible. Satan had blurred my vision and I could not see the truth. I only knew that God had not delivered as He promised me. Then, as I looked back some 10 years later, I realized that a pact is between two or more people. It can be written or verbal. This agreement was neither written nor verbal because I did not wait for God to answer. I thought that He would heal my brother because of my trust and belief in Him. Wow, was I wrong.

I was trying to bargain with God when I did not have any clout or collateral to be in such a position. I immediately pleaded with God to forgive me for my blind and selfish nature. I was only thinking about my pain and hurt. I had overlooked the pain and hurt God must have felt from my rejection. The Holy Spirit took my mind back to that awful day under the dogwood tree when I rejected God. Tears began to form in my eyes. I was convicted for my selfishness and I fell to my knees, begging God's forgiveness. Even now, as I recall that unforgettable day, hot tears stream down my face and my heart skips a beat. Although I know that God has forgiven me, He keeps this memory fresh in my mind as a reminder of what I could have lost by hardening my heart. I never heard God agree with me. I took His love for me for granted and believed that because of that love, He would do anything I asked of Him.

I know now that I will never blame God again for these strokes and will never try to bargain with Him again. I do know that I must increase my faith before I go before Him. Then I remembered that faith comes by hearing the word of God (*Romans 10:17*). Faith ushers in the possibility of all things. It is through the activation of faith that we can receive the Holy Spirit. Once I understood this principle, *"Faith comes by hearing the word of God,"* I understood my mistake in thinking that God agreed with me. I had not heard the word of God say that my brother would be healed. God had not spoken or revealed it to me nor had a vision appeared to me of his healing. I longed to know more about God's Spirit.

My mother taught me how to pray for spiritual wisdom. I enjoyed the confidential talks we had. I could talk to her about anything. She brought me closer to God by teaching me to believe in myself and in the power of prayer. My eyes were opened. My faith began to increase. I eagerly awaited our quiet times together when she spoke to me about God's wisdom and understanding. I followed her everywhere. I truly loved and admired her.

After the stroke, I sat in my bedroom day after day, looking out my window. This brought back memories of the freedom I enjoyed walking upon God's green earth every day and breathing His air. These were things I took for granted. I never hated or blamed God for my condition. I found myself loving Him more and understanding why sickness, pain and spiritual death happen. They happen so that God may be glorified. God will receive the glory when I am able to walk out of this room and enter the pulpit again. I know Satan is the author of pain, sickness and death. He approached God concerning me, just as He did with Job, and asked God for permission to try me. I told Satan, I am going to come through this trial as pure as Gold. God will receive the victory from this battle. When I went to sleep, God showed me deeper secrets about the spirit world. I recognize today, that despite my rejection of God, during my youth, He honored the conditions of my promise to serve and obey Him. God showed me that Satan spreads a blanket of disbelief over us and places a brick wall before our eyes. We fall victim to his lies and deceptions because he convinces us that we can never penetrate through that brick wall. He further convinces us that we have no power. He uses ministers and false teachers who are not called or chosen by God to do the work for him. My faith in God was coming back and I did not want to put myself in that position again during my youth, where He had to test and prove my trust in Him. That was my first introduction to spiritual warfare. It was my first lesson on the battlefield of my mind.

Now, I must find out from Him again how to protect my mind from these evil thoughts that had led me astray during my youth. I must learn how to cover myself from evil and deception. I will pray to God again that He will allow His Holy Spirit to reveal these secrets to me. I will pray that the Holy Spirit will open my mind and increase my understanding of Him and give me the spirit of discernment. I am going through a stage of rebirth again. God began to give me dreams and visions.

I received a vision from God and He said, "The world is sending out so many scriptural fetuses and they, like the dew from the Sahara Desert, will last a short time." He continued to say, "Travesty, travesty."

Figure 3

I began to run scriptural references on all my dreams and visions to see if they were from God. I searched the Bible to see if my visions were lining up with the Scriptures. I found that this vision lined up with **2 Corinthians 11:13-15 (NIV)**.

In other words, God is saying that He did not call or choose the false preachers who are here now and are yet to be born. Yes, they know the Scriptures very well and can quote them verbatim. However, the key to understanding the vision is that God is not sending the false preachers. He said, "The WORLD is sending them and because the WORLD is sending them, they will not last long." He referred to them as false teachers, false prophets, and false preachers. He said it is a travesty that false prophets are deceiving His people. In **2 Cor. 11: 13-15 (NIV)**, Paul called the false preachers counterfeits of the real thing, dishonest practitioners masquerading as the messengers of Christ. When I consider how Satan himself masquerades as an angel of light, it is only to be expected that his agents shall have the appearance of ministers of righteousness. However, they will get what they deserve in the end. I knew that I was not being deceived by Satan. This was truly God speaking to me. The Holy Spirit had answered my prayers and He was teaching me how to discern the good and the evil in people in high places.

The Origin of Faith and Spiritual Warfare

As I searched the Scriptures for the meaning of faith and where it came from, I was drawn closer to God. My faith increased, and I spoke healing Scriptures and included my name in the verses. My fingers began to move first, then my speech, and my arms. I found that faith began with Abraham, who left his home and family to serve God. I continued to trace faith from the paths of Abraham to the book of Hebrews, which defined faith as our confidence in what we hope for, along with a promise that we will receive the things which we do not see. I also discovered that we were not born with faith like we are born with our instincts and five senses. I found that faith is a spiritual gift from God.

I also learned that Jesus is the author and finisher of our faith. In other words, our faith is in Jesus Christ, who God sent into the world to shape, mold and nurture our belief in Him. He alone will complete the faith which He has written within us. No one can give this faith to another, nor can it be purchased or sold to another.

I found that spiritual warfare was used throughout the Scriptures. I also discovered that spiritual warfare began in Heaven. It started between the angels. **Jude 1:6 (KJV)**, records an argument where Lucifer (Satan) made accusations against Jesus concerning the body of Moses. Michael, the archangel, did not entertain a conversation with Lucifer. Michael rebuked Satan and he fled from him. Then in **Rev. 12:7,** Michael and the heavenly host of angels refused to allow Satan to remain in heaven because he was openly accusing Jesus. They fought Satan and the angels who followed him and threw them out of Heaven. They fell to earth and lived in darkness until God created the world. Satan saw God's creation and decided to get even with God by destroying the man and woman He had created.

Eve was the first earthly human introduced to warfare. It was Eve's ignorance of spiritual warfare that allowed an evil spirit to enter her mind and body. Satan approached Eve in the Garden of Eden with a deceptive scheme to confuse, deceive and destroy God's creation and His plan of immortality for all mankind. Eve was captivated by Satan's voice, his knowledge of the garden and his knowledge of her Creator. Satan knew how to appeal to Eve's primitive intellect and how to approach her without her partner. He had watched her from afar and knew when she would be alone. He would not dare approach her in the presence of Adam because Adam would be more perceptive of his ways.

No doubt, Eve's faith was weak. It is true that God did not speak directly to Eve to command her to keep the garden. Eve did not have a relationship of faith and trust with God. Therefore, she was not committed to the covenant between Adam and God.

Figure 4

The command was given to Adam, but because she was Adam's helpmate, she had a commitment to obey God. There is no record of a personal conversation between Eve and God until after she had given the fruit to Adam. Eve was not always with Adam when God spoke to him. All the knowledge of God and His plan came directly from her husband. Since God had given Adam dominion over the Garden of Eden, He looked to Adam to carry out His commands. Eve received this command secondhand. Her commitment to Adam demanded her devotion to him and not Satan. God's attention was focused on Adam and He looked to Adam for an explanation of why the agreement concerning the Tree of Knowledge was broken. God trusted Adam. His faith, until the point where he touched and ate the fruit, was always solid and consistent with God's plan. However, when Eve, possibly with provocation and feminine desires, (remember she was wise now), approached Adam, he was weak and accepted the lie and deception with her. Before Adam reversed his role of authority with Eve, there was a bond of creator and humanity, teacher, and student, lover, and friend, between Adam and God. That kind of relationship would never be duplicated again. The bonds were broken. The faith and trust God had placed in Adam stretched beyond the limit of our imagination, they were meant to last forever.

God finally speaks to Eve, **(Gen..3:13)**, *"What is this you have done?"* The woman said, *"The serpent tricked me, and I ate."* When we lose faith and trust, we look to find a scapegoat for the reason why faith left us. Eve knew that what she did was wrong, that is why she blamed Satan. Eve disobeyed her husband and God. She jeopardized Adam's role as a leader and keeper of the garden. Therefore, God had to put them out of the garden. They left the garden stripped of their identities, ashamed of their interactions, and naked of their innocence. They were originally sinless and not responsible for their actions. Now, their deeds, good and bad, rested upon their shoulders, the shoulders of their children and of all mankind. Adam looked at Eve in an unnatural and desirous way that he never looked at her before. He was now looking at a woman with desires and a single mind of her own.

Figure 5

Let's examine for a moment, the location of the trees. It is amazing that the Tree of Life and the Tree of Knowledge of Good

and Evil were in the center of the Garden of Eden. All the other trees were located throughout the garden. Adam and Eve were told they could touch and eat the fruit of all the trees in the garden except the Tree of Knowledge. Evidently, the other trees did not have the power of these two trees. Let us also remember that the first five books of the Bible are called the Torah and were written in Hebrew before the present interpretation (English language). Symbolism was often used to represent heavenly, earthly and human beings.

In the Hebrew language, the word trees represented people. The limbs are their arms and the trunks are their bodies and legs. Therefore, we may gather that the two trees in the center of the garden as well as the other trees had human forms. One of the two trees had the form of Satan (the tree of the knowledge of good and, evil, emotions as well as sexual and perverted desires). Satan knew right from wrong, that was evident in his quest to deceive Eve and expose her to all these emotions and sexual desires. The other tree (the Tree of Life) was in the form of God because it had healing qualities and everlasting life. Eve was overcome by the words spoken from The Tree of Knowledge (Satan) because it entangled her emotions and introduced her to feelings she'd never felt with Adam. She felt empowered and had to introduce these sexual desires to Adam, who engaged in these desires with Eve and lost his sense of direction. All the bonds Adam shared with God were now broken.

According to Brown, Driver, and Briggs, "Adam and Eve's eyes were open to know right from wrong." The bond between creator and humanity was broken. What Adam and Eve were experiencing was the effects of sin. They had sinned. Sin causes shame and loss of self- respect. It causes a person to feel unclean and dirty. Not only had they lost self-respect for each other, but God had lost respect and trust in them. The bond of teacher and student was broken. They quickly saw their naked bodies and were ashamed to look at God and each other.

They placed their faith in what Satan had tricked them into believing and finally, the bond of lover and friend was broken. They threw everything God had told them out the window and believed the lies and words of Satan. There was a breach in faith. There was enmity between God and Adam that was cast down through generations. Losing one's faith has consequences. It causes us to see ourselves in a different light, one that is dull and opaque. It causes us to hide from the truth and those who are carriers of the truth. It causes us to always be doubtful of our trust in anyone and anything. Adam lost his faith in God and God could not trust him again with His creation. Adam and Eve had to leave the garden. God had prepared an eternal place of everlasting life and continual rest for mankind. All Adam had to do was have faith and trust in God. He never asked Adam to pray to Him or bow down to Him. All He asked of Adam was to replenish (recharge) and take care of the trees in the Garden. Adam's loss of God's trust and faith was devastating. It took away the gift of everlasting life for mankind and his rule over the animal kingdom. It gave the woman an everlasting life of painful childbearing years, it gave man eternal work for his living. It introduced into the world, an evil spirit that lives within the hearts and minds of mankind and created internal conflict. Finally, it caused God to look elsewhere for someone who could take Adam's place.

Faith comes directly from having a personal relationship with God. That relationship is made known to the believer when he/she develops a personal relationship with the Holy Spirit. Why the Holy Spirit? The Holy Spirit teaches us all things. He counsels and seals us.

The seal of the Holy Spirit means that He keeps us near the empty cross where Satan can never touch us. The Holy Spirit is the Spirit of the Living God, and because God lives, the Holy Spirit also lives. He was here in the beginning with God before the earth was formed. **Gen.1:2** *And the Spirit of God was upon the face of the waters.* He was also with God and Jesus as **Gen.1:26,** *Let us make man in our image, after our likeness.*

The Holy Spirit was created in all of us. We are all created in the image of God the Father; God the Son; and God the Holy Spirit. The Bible calls this trinity of deities the Godhead. The word Trinity does not appear in the Bible. Man coined the word because of the three forms of God. Sin has blinded us so that we are unable to see or recognize these forms in ourselves or others. This blind state of mind was developed by Satan to separate us from our creator, just as he separated Adam and Eve from the presence of God. If we are not focused on God, Satan can destroy our souls.

Below is a representation of the Godhead:

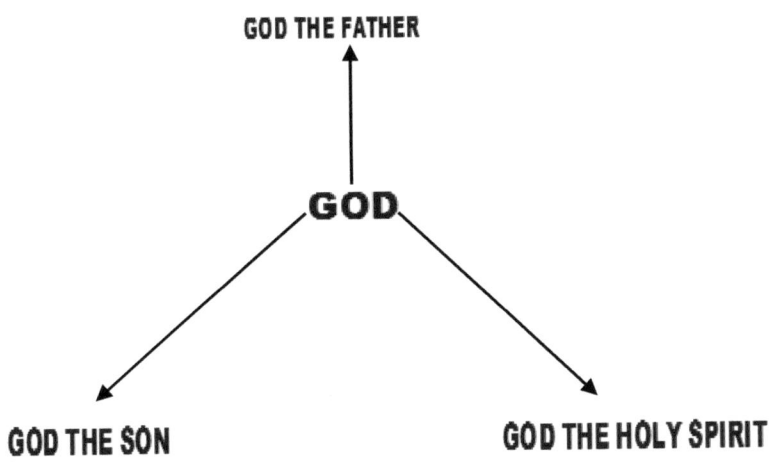

Figure 6

God can appear as himself, as Jesus, and as the Holy Ghost. Some churches leave out the Father and the Holy Spirit and use Jesus only to represent all three. The only problem with that approach is that they are negating the purpose and work of each deity. The Father draws, **John 6:44 (KJV)** the Son saves, **Luke**

19:10 (**KJV**) and the Holy Spirit seals **Eph. 1:13** (**KJV**). Most people, when they hear of the threefold works of God, ask the questions, "How can God be three persons in one?" How do we know which one to worship and who to pray to?" We worship all, but we pray to God, the Father, in the name of Jesus in the presence of the Holy Spirit.

When teaching the Godhead to Bible classes, I often make references to myself, as a classroom teacher, a parent, and a Bible teacher. I, the classroom teacher, the parent and the Bible teacher are all the same person but serve in three different capacities. I, as a classroom teacher, cannot teach the same concepts to my class that I teach to my Bible class. In other words, Jesus cannot seal, (because He saves) nor the Holy Ghost draws (because He seals), and God draws.

Each deity has a different role in God's plan of salvation for mankind and must exercise their authority in those positions. The concept of the three-in-one, also known as the Trinity, must be fully understood before we can receive or know what it means to be full of the Holy Spirit.

We must know the work and purpose of each person in the Trinity (Godhead).

We cannot practice losing and binding because we need the assistance of the Godhead. There is evidence throughout the Scriptures that support the Godhead. **Colossians 2:9** (**KJV**) *"For in Him (Jesus) dwells all the fullness of the Godhead bodily."* God may also appear as the Father of Jesus. **Romans 15:6** (**KJV**), speaks of the Father as God, *"That ye may with one mind and one mouth, glorify God, even the Father of our Lord Jesus Christ."* **Hebrews 1:8** (**KJV**), Jesus is called God, *"But unto the Son, He saith, Thy throne, O God, is for ever and ever: a sceptre of righteousness is the sceptre of thy kingdom."*

The Primary Weapons of Spiritual Warfare

The substance is the primary ingredient in faith. The substance is the energy that pushes the force and drives the mind, telling it to run when the body wants to give up. The substance gives encouragement when all other sources of strength have left the mind and the body. The substance is the burning fire in warfare that assures us that we will receive the things we hope, dream and have visions of. The substance is the light that keeps burning when darkness is all around us. It is the glowing feeling of victory in the battle, though we did not fight the war.

Hebrews 11:1 *"Now faith is the substance of things hoped for, the evidence of things not seen."* The only way we can receive the things we hope for is through the Holy Spirit. The evidence is the proof, confirmation and the substantiation of what the Holy Spirit has done. When we see the reality of things appear and do not know how they got here or where they came from, that is evidence. Evidence is witnessing the impossible become a possibility.

Evidence is the results of spiritual warfare. When we see someone escape death, get up from their sick bed, get a job that they did not apply for or a house they did not purchase, we can say that these facts are the results of warfare. The evidence or results of spiritual warfare is when we witness someone, out of the blue, fall on their knees, crying and giving their life to Christ. The evidence of things not seen is the results of warfare. It is the proof that the Holy Spirit is at work in the lives of the believer. The evidence of unseen things is constantly manifested all around us.

Faith eliminates possibilities of how these things could happen or where they came from. Faith does not question spiritual things, but presents the results, whether natural or unnatural.

Figure 7

It is crucial for to fully understand the fruits, gifts, and work of the Holy Spirit so that He will be effective in our lives. It is also important that believers are fully anointed and confident to do the works that God has called us to do. We cannot be effective as a doer for God if we do not know how to defend ourselves against our enemies or understand the weapons of our warfare. Just as a soldier is prepared to use his weapons to fight the enemy, the believer is given the same instructions.

2 Corinthians 10:4 *"For the weapons of our warfare are not carnal, but mighty through God for the pulling down of strongholds."* In other words, Paul is saying, we who are Christians do not fight our enemies physically. Our weapons are much more powerful because they come directly from God, who is the creator of all things. Furthermore, we are not looking for flesh and blood to destroy our enemies. We destroy them with the powerful spiritual gifts that the Holy Spirit gives to the believer.

The demonstration of the Holy Spirit is given to all men for the common good **1 Cor.12:7**. In other words, there is a propensity to do well in all men because the Holy Spirit is available to all who will receive Him. We must recognize Him and be receptive to Him when He speaks to us.

The nine fruits of the Holy Spirit listed in **Galatians 5:22-23:**
- *love*
- *joy*
- *peace*
- *longsuffering*
- *gentleness*
- *goodness*
- *faith*
- *meekness*
- *temperance*

The nine spiritual gifts taken from **1 Corinthians 12:8:**
- *wisdom*
- *knowledge*
- *faith*
- *healing*
- *miracles*
- *prophecy*
- *discerning of spirits*
- *speaking in tongues*
- *interpreting tongues*

Rarely does a person have all the gifts. The prophets of old and certain disciples of Jesus had all these gifts. That is why they were effective at using spiritual warfare. Practitioners of spiritual warfare today are weak because they fail to spend precious time in the presence of the Holy Spirit. Many people believe that they will never get as close to God as His disciples were. This is not true. Paul met Jesus after His death and had a closer walk with God than any of His disciples. Jesus anointed and spoke directly to him on the road to Damascus. That is why he was called an apostle. He sent him to Ananias where he could receive further training about His works and the works of the Holy Spirit.

Faith warriors possessing these gifts are truly powerful and effective. Notice, faith is found as a fruit and a gift of the Holy Spirit. That within itself is revealing and powerful. It is revealing because we now know why faith is important and why **Hebrews 11:6**, *without faith, it is impossible to please God*. This is the only fruit and gift in which this declaration is made. Faith is powerful because it has capabilities of bringing into existence things that do not exist into the realm of reality just by believing and speaking the words.

Faith is powerful and there is no fear of the enemy. The enemy can feel the anointing of a person with faith because it is the fruit and gift of the Holy Spirit. He can smell the sweet spirit lingering because releasing the aroma of a ripe fruit is what faith, love, and the other fruits emanate.

> **FAITH** *releases a* **SWEET, SWEET SPIRIT** *that shackles fear and doubt*

Faith is above reproach for the enemy or a non-believer seeking to cast doubt in the hearts and minds of the believer. The enemy stays a great distance from them and skillfully watches all their movements, waiting for an opening whereby he may attack and destroy them.

We are able, through faith, to pull down strongholds Satan has placed upon us and our loved ones. Strongholds are any weakness that Satan uses to keep us in bondage. The bonds and shackles of fear, doubt and confusion are strongholds.

Anytime we cannot make sound and stable decisions, Satan is at work, convincing us that the decisions we are about to make will harm us, take away our identity, or cause us to lose authority over a person, situation or position. Once we become rooted and grounded in faith, we are more than conquerors. Our enemies will try to defeat us, but our countenance, faith, and confidence in who we are will sustain us. Once the enemy recognizes that he has no power over our anointing, he becomes powerless and must release our loved ones. Our enemies are peculiar in that they never forget what we have done to them. They may not speak or look directly at us, but they are constantly lurking in the background waiting for us to slip, make a mistake or fall.

A good Scripture to memorize is **Isaiah 54:17**, *no weapon formed against me shall prosper and every tongue that rises against me in judgment, I shall condemn.* The fruits and gifts are alike in that they come directly from the Holy Spirit. They are powerful and equip the believer with strength, confidence, and belief that he/she will conquer and perform those tasks for which he/she has been called. They are assurances to the believer that he/she is not alone and when they go to war, there are ten thousand angels waiting to protect and defend them on all sides (**Psalm 91:11**). These fruits and gifts are spiritual weapons against the enemy because the enemy cannot love unconditionally; he cannot dwell in peace with contentment. He can never experience the excitement that joy brings. This excitement comes from knowing that we are pleasing God. The enemy has no intentions of loving or pleasing God. The enemy has no knowledge of longsuffering, gentleness, goodness, meekness, and self-control because he is the author of the opposite of these fruits. He operates in the opposing realm of what the Holy Spirit specializes in. The enemy only pretends to have the power to frighten us into submission.

When my siblings and I were young, we were afraid of the dark and would run and hide because we were afraid of the "Boogieman." My mother would console us by telling us that the "Boogieman" was like an old lion that had no teeth and could not bite. All he could do was roar and scare people. She said the people who believed that he was dangerous fell in his den and were trapped by him. She would always say, "Call on Jesus when you are scared, and He will come and save you." I believed those words as a child, but when I grew older, I forget them and seldom called on Jesus. I decided to live a good life and raise my children the same way. Little did I know that one day I would come face to face with Satan and would not remember these precious words my mother told us.

As the years passed, I continued to have visions and would wake up at night in cold sweats. I tried to fight the visions but the more I fought, the more visions I had. I often had visions of warplanes. I had visions of the horses spoken of in the book of Revelations and Jesus Himself speaking and warning me of things that would come to pass. This gift was like a millstone around my neck because I did not know how to deal with it. The more speaking engagements I accepted, the bigger the void became in my life. I knew I was not doing what God had called me to do. The final straw was broken when I had a vision of my death and I was leaving my body going to be with my loved ones. I saw my spirit leave my body and linger above my bed, looking down upon my body as I lay there beside my husband.

Figure 8

It was a weird feeling. I had never had an out of body experience and even the memory of it is still fresh in my mind. I thought that I was leaving this world, but, not as I had believed I would go. I had no time to talk to my husband or my children. I had no time to think about tomorrow or what my children would do without me.

Then, quickly, my spirit took off and I was in space, among the stars, moving fast toward a bright wide light. I saw my aunts among the stars, beckoning me to come on. There were smiles, peace, and contentment upon their faces. I felt so relaxed and peaceful.

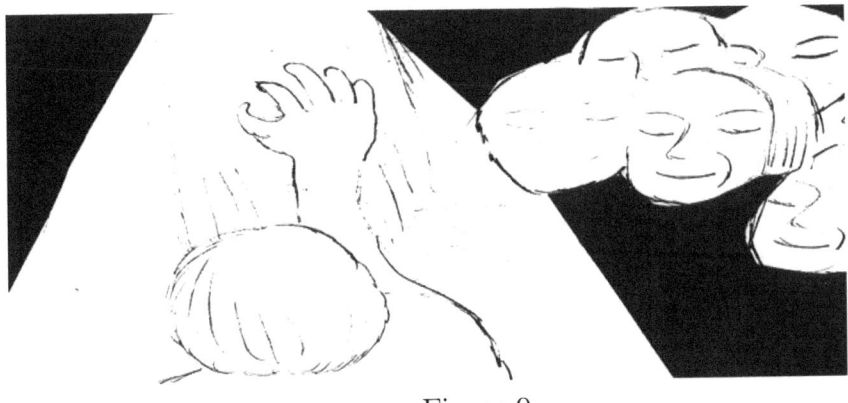

Figure 9

My spirit slowed down and I began to feel a glow of warmth covering my entire body. Abruptly, my spirit stopped, and I knew I was in the presence of the Lord. I said, "Precious Lord, take my hand." Instantly, I felt my spirit go backward. It was moving backward just as fast as it had moved forward. I was back in my body in my bed. My head was throbbing, but I was alive. I felt my blood rushing through my veins as if my veins would burst. I told my husband about the experience. We both thanked God that I had returned. I went to work that morning. My pressure was extremely high because I could still hear my blood rushing through my body. I went to the nurse's office to have my pressure read. I was expecting her to call the ambulance, but she said, "Your pressure is perfect." The only person I told was my husband.

THE STRUGGLE TO PREACH IS THE CALL OF SPIRITUAL WARFARE
Chapter 2

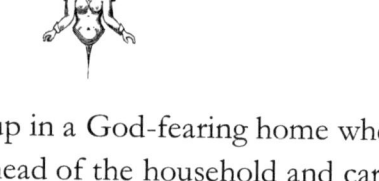

I was brought up in a God-fearing home where the male was the head of the household and carried out all the leadership roles in the home. We looked to our father for strength and endurance in worldly matters, but we looked to our mother for matters of the heart, spiritual food, and religious teachings.

After living through the vision of my spirit among the stars, the call to preach weighed heavily on my heart. Maybe that was what God was preparing me for. I tried to squash it by refusing to listen to the inner voice that was always whispering in my ear. I carried those hidden thoughts in my heart from the time I was six years old until I was married and had grown children. Several times I heard the call, but because of tradition, I never discussed it with my mother. I truly needed her but she was no longer with me. She would tell me what to do. Although I had dreams and visions of her, she never discussed my role as a preacher.

Then the call became so great that I could not hide it any longer. I found myself straying from my prepared messages to exaltations of God. I always had a deep desire to go further and preach, but, I contained myself and shut down my burning desire to preach. I often saw myself in my dreams preaching before large congregations. I even saw myself wearing a robe and standing behind a pulpit, but I never had the courage to pursue those dreams. I thought that speaking about God's word would be enough to please Him, but talking about God only wet my appetite to feed the burning inferno growing inside of me.

I had to get this fire out of me, but I had no one to talk to. My mother had been dead for 12 years and my father did not believe in women preachers. My husband never thought of me as a preacher and my son was not looking forward to being ridiculed by his friends. I was like a leaf blowing in the wind. There was nowhere I could land and feel safe and secure, so I kept floating. I knew that something had to happen quickly before I exploded. I was unhappy and felt the displeasure of God as I tried to run away from Him.

The Vision from God

I fell asleep while sitting in my den on New Year's Eve night in 1991. I was waiting for my husband to come home from Night Watch. He was elected pastor of a local church in the community. Serving as the First Lady was a challenging duty because I was expected to follow my husband to all the church functions. I was tired that night, so I decided to stay home and wait up for him, but soon as I sat on the couch, I fell into a deep sleep. I was instantly swept up into a cloud where I met a woman with a shawl over her head and shoulder. She asked me, "Why are you afraid to preach God's holy word?" I told her that because I was a woman, no one would listen to me. She took me by the hand and said, "Come with me." We were carried up into billowing clouds where she showed me Jesus hanging on the cross.

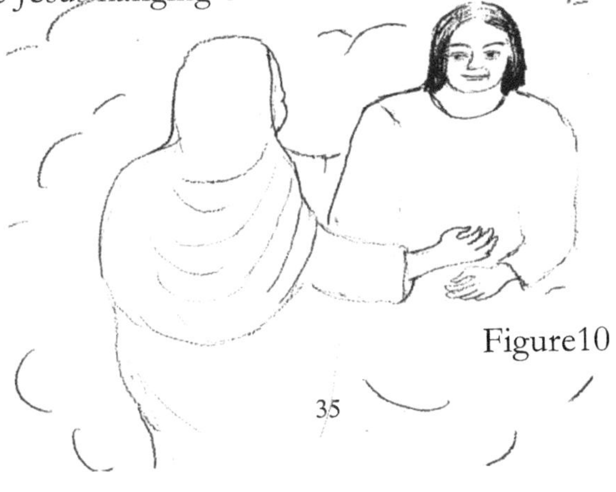

Figure 10

Figure 11

She said, "Look, look what they are doing to my Son. They are still hammering nails into His hands and feet; they are still piercing Him in His side." I cried and said to her, "But I am just a woman, they will never listen to me." Then I was standing along. White billowing clouds were forming in the sky. I looked up and I saw a white horse with a warrior sitting on him. The rider had a bright shining sword in His hand.

Figure 12

He was so bright that to look upon him caused my eyes to burn. I fell on my knees with my head tucked in my arms and my hands over my head. He said, "Arise child." I stood up trembling. He said, "Hold out your right hand." I was trembling, but I did exactly what He said. I held my hand out, looked up and saw a sword so sharp and bright that was about to fall upon my hand. I thought it would cut my hands into pieces, but when it gently touched my hands, it quickly turned into a Bible. I heard Him say, "Go Preach My Gospel."

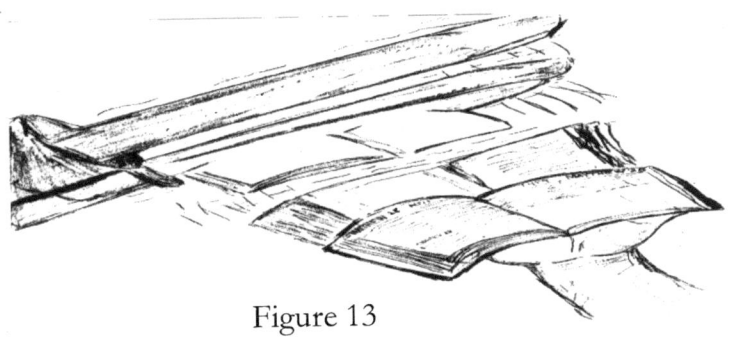

Figure 13

I told the dream to my husband and we both cried. He said that he would consult the deacons in the church and set up a date for me to preach my initial sermon. I knew that I could not run anymore. I had been running for 20 years and now it was time to stop. They chose the second Sunday in March for my initial sermon. I told one other person, a well-known evangelist, about my dream. She advised me not to tell anyone because people would think I was crazy if I told them I had spoken to Mary and Jesus. She said that it was a trick of Satan. So, I kept the vision of my calling to the ministry in the closet for over 25 years. I had a yearning to be obedient to God, but I kept hearing her voice.

The initial sermon was two weeks away. I began to long for my mother. If she was only here, she would tell me exactly what to do. She would tell me if my vision was from God or the devil. I was truly torn. I wanted to run away and hide. I knew it was the enemy trying to scare me, but, I needed to talk with someone who could remove this blanket of doubt from my eyes.

A Message from a Deceased Pastor

I wanted to talk to my mother about preaching, but, that was impossible, so I decided to talk to my father. My father was a strong-willed man who was raised on traditional customs and beliefs. Rarely did he change his mind about things he was rooted and grounded in. I knew how he felt and what he would say, but I told him anyway. He said that he did not believe women were born to preach because it wasn't in the Bible.

Then he said, "Are you sure that God called you to preach?" I did not tell him about the vision, but I did tell him that God said, "Go preach my Gospel." He finally said, "Well, if that is what you think you heard, I reckon you have no choice, but to go." I did not like his choice of the word, if, because to me, the word implied doubt, and his response raised more doubt in my mind. I had no one, except my husband, to talk to.

Other ministers were questioning my husband to find out if he was really going to let his wife preach. My husband said, "I will not stand between her and God. She said God said go preach His Gospel, and I believe her." I went to bed that night, but my mind went elsewhere. I dreamed about my first pastor, Rev. E.W. Wright, who introduced me to God through his preaching. He was the first to baptize me when I was eight years old. I truly loved and respected him. He was my pastor from my birth to his death.

He watched me grow from a baby to a young woman. He was there when I finished high school, went off to college, and got my first teaching job. He was also there when I got married, and even when I had my first child. He asked my husband to serve under him after his initial sermon because he did not want me to leave the church. He preached my brother's and mother's funerals. He loved me as if I was his child. He had always been like a second father to me and here he was again at my lowest point in life.

He told me to believe in myself and not to let others, who do not know God, sway me from trusting God. He asked me, "Didn't God bring you this far?" I said, "Yes He did." He said, "Then why would you doubt Him now?"

He continued, "Be grateful and honored that He came to you and bestowed this gift upon you. Go and use it. You will see that He will never fail you. Trust God and count it all joy," he added. Rev Wright visited me every night up until the day of my initial sermon. We walked together around the yard of the old wooden church and he gave me pointers on how to preach effectively. He said, "Don't try to hoop. Most preachers think of it as putting gravy on the meat, but what good is the gravy if there is no meat?" He encouraged me to be real and said that if I was real, God would be real with me.

Figure 14

He taught me how to sing old hymns and said hymns will warm

up a cold audience. He told me to research my topic to see what was happening in the area during that time and make it relevant to today. He said, "Never use mail ordered sermons. Always write your own; someone may say they heard another minister preach the same sermon." Then he said, "If you ever pastor a church, never become indebted to the members."

When Rev. Wright said God was Real, I felt relieved and comfortable because when I heard God say, "Go preach my Gospel," it was also real. When I went to bed the next night, God gave me the title of my sermon and where to find it in the Bible. The subject He gave me was, "When the Morning Comes," from *2 Chronicles 16-17*.

When the hour arrived that afternoon, the church was packed. Many people came out of curiosity to see the first women in the association preach. The row in the back of the church was lined with ministers from the association. I was introduced by a friend who was an ordained pastor and lawyer from Knoxville, Tenn. I greeted the audience, read the Scriptures and gave the background of the Scriptures.

Then I gave my subject. I did not need any notes because God was whispering in my ear telling me what to say. The members of the audience were up on their feet. The preachers from the back came to the front and were in amazement. The Holy Spirit moved all over the church, even in the pulpit. There was not a dry eye anywhere. God showed up and convicted the non-believers that He truly sent me.

My father was convicted and said, "When she came and told me she had been called to preach, I asked her was she sure that God had called her? I will never ask her again because I am a witness to what God has done." All the ministers made comments like my father. God had made believers of all the doubters.

I thanked Rev. Wright who was there in the spirit. He really trained me good and gave me some lasting advice. I will always hold him in high regards because he came back from the grave to help renew my trust and faith in God when I needed it most. I have never heard from him again through my dreams or visions, but I am sure that I will hear from him again when I come to another turning point in my life. I thanked God for His Holy Spirit and how He used me to spread His Gospel to His people.

My father confided in me some years later, before his death, that God had called him to preach several years before I was born, but he declined the call. He said he regretted not answering that call. He said that was why he wanted me to be sure that the call was real. Instead of answering the call to preach, my dad settled for being a devout deacon in the church for over 60 years.

My father was an astute Bible teacher and always kept my husband and me on our toes when it came to righteous living and knowing the Bible. He lived to be 94 years old before God finally called him home.

My husband and I stayed with him during the night. We asked him questions when we needed a reference from the Bible. He was always right. I saw a vision of his death during the Christmas holidays. This was God's way of preparing me for his departure. I was asleep in the upper bedroom when I heard a crashing noise outside and the clanging of metal bells along the road. I saw the rocking chair my father sat in overturned on the floor.

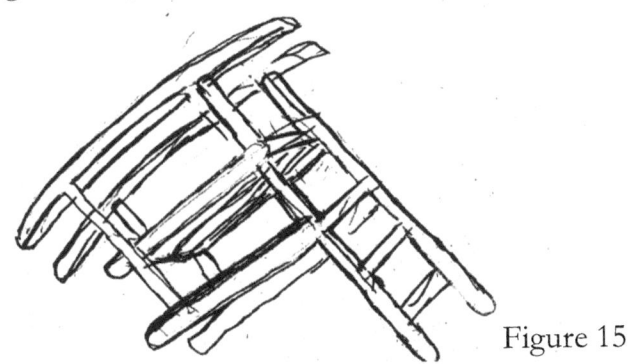

Figure 15

My focus was fixed on the rocking chair. I knew there was

some symbolism in the chair being overthrown. The chair was a symbol of authority in the house. It was the highest chair and the only chair that exemplified comfort, stability, and control. The fact that this chair was on its head was an indication of the future state of things to come in this house. A few seconds later, the noise was inside the house coming up the hallway. I was shaking with fear. Finally, the noise stopped at my father's room. My focus shifted from the rocking chair to the noise. The noise was a symbol of disarray, disorganization, and chaos.

I knew what was in store for all the children raised in this home. It was the death angel telling me that my father would soon leave us and would no longer give us instructions and words of wisdom concerning our lives. It was the month of December. I began to play Christmas music while trimming the tree. My father was sad during the days that followed the vision. He was sitting in the room with me and told me where all the lights and ornaments were stored. He sang along with the music. Suddenly, he broke down in tears. He said that this would be his last Christmas with us. I went to him, held him in my arms and we both cried together.

The situation was worsening when my husband was found at home by our son in an unconscious state. He was rushed to the hospital and ended up in the intensive care unit. I tried to take care of two homes, my father's and my husband's. My father was sad during the days that followed. Then, the unforgettable happened. I decided to stay at home one night because I was exhausted. I traded places with my sister who stayed with our father. I received a call from her late in the night that our father had fallen. We rushed him to the hospital and discovered that he had a broken hip. My husband was in one hospital and my father was in another hospital across town.

Snow was on the ground and was still falling while I was in the Intensive Care Unit with my husband. I was torn between staying with my husband and going to see my father. I decided to drive in the snow to see my father. When I got there, my sister was getting ready to leave because of the amount of snow that had fallen on the ground.

    I stood at the foot of the bed with my sister and the floor nurse. I saw my father's eyes had a glaze over them. He could not talk, but his eyes followed me around the room as if he was trying to say something to me. He knew that this would be his last time with us. His eyes spoke for him. I went over to his bedside to kiss him for the last time. I left him knowing that I had to see my husband before the snow covered the roads.

Figure 16

RECEIVING THE KEY TO SPIRITUAL WARFARE
Chapter 3

Although I knew how to preach, I continue to believe that I was being equipped for something else. I do not recall any other preacher, man or woman, talk about any of their visions and how they could see into the future. I never heard anyone speak of their calling as vivid as my calling. I read my Bible daily, but I felt that I was missing something that I couldn't quite put my finger on. As I was getting closer to God, Satan was moving closer to me. I did not know how to stop him, I tried praying, but something was missing. He was not leaving me alone. He would allow me to taste victory and then he would snatch it from me. I wanted it to stop.

One night I had a terrible vision that I was walking alone in an open valley. The entire surrounding was dark, so dark that it was a thick and velvety blackness. I could not even see my hands or feet. As I stumbled through the darkness, I heard something walking behind me. I started walking faster. The faster I walked the louder and quicker the steps got. Whatever was behind me was getting closer. My heart was pounding so hard, like the sound of kettle drums. My legs felt like mush. My feet were like lead blocks. They just would not move. I was frozen in my tracks. I was afraid to run, so I abruptly stopped. When I stopped, something quickly jumped on me from behind. The weight of it was so heavy that it brought me crashing to the ground. I had no idea what was happening, but it was scaring me so bad that I had trouble breathing. Once I felt the life draining from my body I immediately knew it was Satan, the dragon and the prince of this world.

    My face was pushed into the soil. I could barely move or breathe. I struggled through the night trying to get away from his grasp. I could feel his horrible breath breathing on my neck. The stench from his body filled my nose with an odor that was nauseating. The mist and vapor from his breath made the hairs on my neck quiver and stand on ends. He was suctioning my breath from me. I felt the life draining from my body. Suddenly, he pushed me deeper into the earth, pinning my hands and arms behind my back. My entire life began to flash before my eyes as I felt my spirit and soul leaving my body. I didn't have the strength to fight. Then, he said, "I am going to hold you here until the sun comes up. When it rises over the horizon, it will be a sign that your soul belongs to me." I struggled to get loose as tears formed in my eyes.

Figure 17

    I just couldn't give up. I screamed until I couldn't hear my voice anymore. My throat was dry and felt like fire on the inside, racing up, down and throughout my body. I felt as if I was in a burning inferno and would have given anything for a cool breeze or a sip of water to cool my body. I knew that Satan was aware of my fears and wanted to scare me, so I would give in to him. I was made aware of his tricks and evil ways during my youth and I refused to allow him to trick me a second time. I just had to hang on until my change would come.

The more I struggled, the stronger his hold was on me. I twisted and turned until my body was tired. I felt drained of all my spiritual substance, but I just couldn't give up. I couldn't give him my soul. I had to fight. I summoned every nerve and fiber in my body to line up with the words of God. I fought him with every ounce of strength in my drained body while hearing his raspy voice breath hot and warm sprints of vapor upon my neck.

My Deceased Mother Gave Me the Key to Spiritual Warfare

I saw the dark began to disappear and the sky was getting lighter. My heart pounded harder and harder. I thought it would burst. Then, out from the grave came the voice of my mother. She said, "Frances, rebuke him." I looked around but did not see anyone. Tears began to fall from my eyes because I wanted my mother with me again. I wanted to feel her arms around me, telling me that everything was all right. I wanted her to fight this battle for me. I screamed, "mamma, help me!" The voice said, "Go ahead and rebuke him, now!" I said, "Satan, I rebuke you," but he held me down much stronger. She said, "No, baby, you must rebuke him in the name of Jesus and he will flee from you. You have power over him by using the name Jesus." I quickly said, "Satan, I rebuke you in the name of JESUS!!!" He began to loosen his grip. I said it again with much more power and authority," Satan, I REBUKE you in the name of JESUS. Satan released my hands and was getting ready to flee when I grabbed his hands, turned around and looked him dead in his eyes.

My mother wanted me to see the enemy. She wanted me to see who and what it was that was fighting me. She wanted me to fear only God who had the power to destroy both body and soul in hell, (**Matt. 10:28**). When I turned around, I saw his hideous face

SPIRITUAL WARFARE

which quickly changed into the faces of men, women, boys, and girls.

I felt empowered, as if I finally knew how to fight him and keep him off my back, away from my home and out of my children's lives. My mother had given me the key to my future. Everything was falling in place now. I finally knew why I was having dreams and visions I did not understand. The vision of Jesus riding a white horse and the sword turning into a Bible became more than real. I finally knew my purpose in life. God was preparing me to be a spiritual warrior and to fight the good fight.

Figure 18

Learning How to Defeat the Enemy

My mother wanted me to know that Satan uses people to do his work. Some of these people I will know because some will be friends and relatives, while others will be people on the job or in the community. She would always tell us when we were children to never look down, "Always look a person in the eye when you speak to them." This is an assurance that you know who your enemies are. Looking people directly in the eye says, "I do not fear you, I know who I am." It also says that you have authority over your situations and circumstances.

The eyes are a mirror to the soul. "The eyes are the lamp of the body. If your eyes are healthy, your whole body will be full of light. But if your eyes are unhealthy, your whole body will be full of darkness. If then the light within you is darkness, how great is that darkness?" **Matt. 6:22-23** (**NIV**).

Having the light and letting it shine is an illumination of your faith. When we have the light in us we can do all things through Jesus Christ who gives us strength. We will react quickly to falsehoods and will defend our trust in God. Since we are faith walkers, nothing and no one can change our minds or cause us to turn our backs on God. We are true to God first and then to ourselves. It is very difficult, almost impossible, to have faith in God when we do not believe in ourselves. Believing in ourselves gives us power over others while believing in Jesus gives us power over demons. There is Power in the Name of Jesus.

I searched the scriptures to see if the word, rebuke, existed and I found it in **Matt. 17:18**, which says, *"And Jesus rebuked him, and the demon came out of him, and the boy was cured at once."* I also read **Mark 9:25** which says, *"When Jesus saw that a crowd was rapidly gathering, He rebuked the unclean spirit, saying to it, "You deaf and mute spirit, I command you, come out of him and do not enter him again."* **Luke 4:41** says, *"Demons also were coming out of many, shouting, 'You are the Son of God!' But rebuking them, He would not allow them to speak because they knew Him to be the Christ."* I found the word, rebuke, throughout the New Testament in relation to spiritual warfare.

Spiritual warfare was not taught in my church during my youth, no more than it is taught today. Many people are afraid of spiritual warfare because of the unclean, evil, demonic and satanic spirits associated with warfare. Many see it as a form of witchcraft because of the demons and the methods of casting out evil spirits. Satan studies his prey and knows their moves, characteristics, personalities, likes, and dislikes. He knows their weaknesses and strengths.

When I was struggling to get away from Satan, his hold on me intensified. I had no strength or power to get away from him. He knew that when he kept me in this position, I could not use my mind or my heart to recall Bible verses to give me strength. My primary focus was on getting out from under the pressure of his traumatic hold, I was broken. I thought that I had lost the battle. Everything inside of me told me that it was finished. I was desperately trying to fight the battle alone. I had no weapons to fight him, and he was aware of this. My life was like dust in his hands. He had the upper advantage. When my mother said to rebuke Satan, she was giving me a key to fight Satan. When she said to rebuke him in the name of Jesus, she was equipping me with the primary weapon to defeat him.

When we are in a battle with Satan, we should never lose our focus. Once we take our focus off God, Satan comes in for the kill. I thank God for sending the voice of my mother to remind me that it is not finished. Her voice was able to break the stronghold that Satan had on me. After the rebuke, I was on the battlefield with my Lord. I was able to regain my strength and focus on Jesus who is my captain. My focus was so strong that it was able to tear down the wall of separation. I was in control of my mind, heart, and soul. These three entities are the nuggets that Satan desires to conquer. Once he has them, it is hard to come back.

There is power in the name of Jesus. **James 4:7 (KJV)** says, *"Submit yourselves therefore to God. Resist the devil, and he will flee from you."* Submit means to place ourselves under God's authority. It also means to get under the covering of God. Knowing your place in God keeps you protected. Resist means to withstand, endure, hold out and do not give in. When we resist the devil, it is like a protective coating. It is just like wax or varnish that is poured over an object to protect its surface from the weather. Knowing your place in Jesus is the primary weapon used in warfare. Once you realize your place, Satan's power is ineffective.

THE WORKS AND TOOLS OF THE HOLY SPIRIT IN SPIRITUAL WARFARE
Chapter 4

Once I gained a personal relationship with God, He opened the door of truth about all things and the Spirit of Truth Himself. I started hearing words buzzing around my ears, words I had never heard before began to fill my mind and heart. I began to write, and the words came to me like water flowing down a mountainside. The words were filled with awe and gave me a feeling of a renewed rebirth of life. I knew I was being filled with the Holy Spirit. Unknown words flowed from my tongue. **John 16: 13-15 (NIV)**, Jesus says, "*But when He, the Spirit of Truth comes, He will guide you into all the truth. He will not speak on His own; He will speak only what He hears, and He will tell you what is yet to come. He will glorify me because it is from me that He will receive what He will make known to you. All that belongs to the Father is mine. That is why I said the Spirit will receive from me what He will make known to you.*" **John 14:16** calls the Holy Spirit a counselor, while **John 16:8-9** says He convicts us of our sins. Then **1 Corinthians 15: 1-4** says He seals us from sin through justification, and **Ephesians 1:13**, says He seals us with the Holy Spirit of promise. **1 Corinthians 3:16**, Paul says, His temple dwells in the believer. If His temple dwells in us, we have confidence and can speak boldly with wisdom and understanding because He speaks for us and through us.

As true believers, should not worry about what we will say when we need to encourage people and assure them of God's comfort, love, and peace. All we should do is open our mouths and the Holy Spirit will speak for us. I had this experience while in college. I had a speech impediment and stuttered while talking. I was in my speech class when the instructor asked me to read Dr. Martin Luther King's speech, "I Have a Dream." My heart sank in my throat. I imagined myself stuttering and running out of the class as I did in high school. It was awful because all the students laughed and made fun at me all through high school. I dreaded talking in public because I could not control my stuttering. However, this day, when I stood up, I felt a sense of strength and confidence come over me as I read the entire speech without stuttering. I felt an anointing filling my heart and moving in my tongue. It was like Dr. King's spirit and voice had entered my body. I felt like chains had been broken from my tongue, my mind, my body and my soul. I felt like a phoenix, rising from the ashes, stretching out his wings and mounting up to fly again. The Holy Spirit had emboldened me and set me free from the chains that had kept me bounded all those years.

Figure 19

Everyone was amazed at my new voice. The class and teacher gave me a standing ovation. I never stuttered again. I was free of Satan's hold on my tongue and mind. I was free to think for myself and to allow God's power to have complete control over my mind, heart, and soul.

Satan has chains with locks on our minds. He wants to be in control. Once we break his hold, we can rise and conquer our fears. *God does not give us a spirit of fear. He gives us power, love, and a sound mind*, **(2 Timothy 1:7).**

Works Are the Expressions of Belief and Love for Jesus

The reader may find several roles and duties of the Holy Spirit, but for the sake of the works, we will list all which are crucial for our battles in spiritual warfare.

The works of the Holy Spirit

- Guides the believer into all truths
- Speaks of what He hears Jesus say
- Reveals to us those things said by Jesus
- Counsels and comforts us
- Seals us through justification
- Brings things to our remembrance
- Seals His words in the temple of our bodies

- Teaches doctrines
- Seals with the Spirit of promise
- Anoints the believer
- Heals the infirmed and broken hearted
- Gives strength and boldness
- Fills the believer with His Spirit
- Glorifies the Father

As you can see, these works are spiritual. Some works, such as strength, boldness, healing, and comfort may appear to be of a physical nature, but the Spirit gives them the power to perform in a physical manner.

The Holy Spirit does not operate in a place where Jesus is not in control. The Holy Spirit is in the form of Jesus when Jesus walked the earth. Jesus spoke only of His Father. Jesus says in **John 12:49,** *"For I have not spoken of myself; but the Father which sent me, He gave me a commandment, what I should say and what I should speak."* The Holy Spirit does not glorify Himself or makes any mention of His power. He only speaks and gives instructions of those things

He hears Jesus say. Since He is the Spirit form of Jesus and God, He knows exactly what they said, when they said it, and the conditions under which the statements were made.

Jesus, while alive, spoke to His disciples when they were in the Upper Room in Jerusalem. He wanted to let them know of His imminent death, but He knew they were not prepared to understand why He had to leave. Therefore, He reassures them of his love. He told them that if they loved Him, He would come back and make Himself known to them. He did just that, in the form of the Holy Spirit. Even this hint was too much for them to grasp.

I have learned that the Holy Spirit is a protective covering that God gives us when we are in Christ and He is in us. This covering is Jesus' way of protecting us from evil and the tricks of Satan. The covering protects us from our head to our feet. Paul calls it a spiritual suit of armor.

My mother taught me this when she said, "There is power in the name of Jesus." She knew that when I called on the name of Jesus, I was instantly covered. It was just like being covered by the blood of Jesus, which is the suit of armor.

The strategy in describing this fight with Satan possibly came to Paul while he was in a Roman prison. The soldiers had on headgear to protect the head and face, along with breastplates to cover the heart and other vital organs. They also wore belts to gird up their loins, shields to protect them from arrows and spears, shoes to protect the feet and a sword to pierce and kill the enemy.

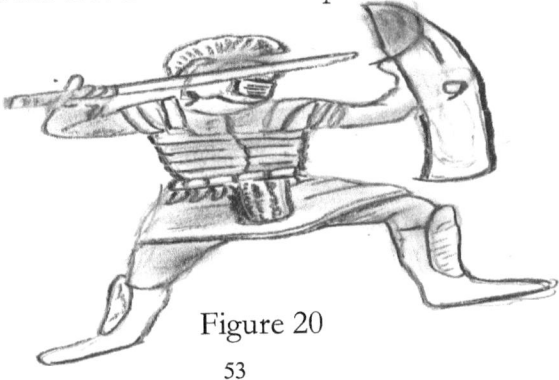

Figure 20

Paul says in **Ephesians 6: 13-18**, *"Therefore, take unto you the whole armor of God, that ye may be able to withstand in the evil day and, having done all, to stand, stand."* The first step in wearing the armor is to know and understand all parts of the armor that God bestows upon the true believer. Paul says, *"Stand, therefore, having your loins girt about with truth, and having on the breastplate of righteousness; And your feet shod with the preparation of the gospel of peace; Above all, taking the shield of faith, wherewith ye shall be able to quench all the fiery darts of the wicked. And take the helmet of salvation, and the sword of the Spirit, which is the word of God: Praying always with all prayer and supplication in the Spirit, and watching thereunto with all perseverance and supplication for all saints."* Knowing all parts of the armor are vital for survival and avoiding the pitfalls of the enemy. Satan will use anything to misrepresent the Scriptures to convince you to remove your armor. However, if you remember that it is not your armor, but the whole armor of God, you will keep it on.

Figure 21

Proofs of the Works of the Holy Spirit

Jesus said to his disciples in **John 14:16-21** that He would pray to the Father and His Father would give them another Comforter who will live with them always and forever. He continues to say that this Comforter, also known as the Spirit of Truth, could not come to the world nor could the world receive Him because they would not be able to see or know who He was. He knew how lost His disciples would be without Him, so He tried to reassure them that He would not leave them alone with no one to comfort or console them. He told them they would not have to wait long, for in just a little while, they would see Him again.

Jesus' disciples, who walked with Him and witnessed all the miracles He performed, had no idea of what He was saying. Then Judas asked Him how He could be shown to them and not to the world? Jesus answered in verses **22-25** (World English Bible), "*If a man loves me, he will keep my word. My Father will love him, and we will come to him, and make our home with him. He who doesn't love me doesn't keep my words. The word which you hear isn't mine, but the Fathers who sent me. I have said these things to you, while still living with you.*" Jesus was using every approach imaginable to assure them that He would come back to them.

Now, I know why my mother read to my brother from the book of John. Jesus said in **John 14:26**, "*But the Comforter, which is the Holy Ghost, whom the Father will send in my name, He shall teach you all things, and bring all things to your remembrance, whatsoever I have said unto you.*" Then, Jesus said to them in **John 14:28-29**, "*Ye have heard how I said unto you, I go away, and come again unto you. If ye loved me, ye would rejoice, because I said, I go unto the Father: for my Father is greater than I. And now I have told you before it comes to pass, that when it is come to pass, ye might believe.*" Notice, Jesus was showing them all the works of the Holy Spirit as He was preparing them to meet Him when He left. He was letting them know that they would never see Him again in the physical form but in His Spirit form. This is proof of His coming.

My mother was teaching and introducing my brother to the Holy Spirit. She knew the Spirit of God. She knew who He was and where He came from. She knew He was the Living Spirit of Jesus who came back just as He promised His disciples. That is why she could take the sight of the blood that was coming from my brother's body. She knew it was temporal. That is why she could smile and hum a song as she washed his soiled clothes. She was engaging in spiritual warfare while at the same time taking care of his physical body. She knew and believed that God was not only preparing a place for him but a new body as well, for his spirit to enter and live again. This is proof of the works of the Holy Spirit in this present time.

My mother understood the connection between prayer and faith. I knew she had an unyielding faith and prayed such passionate prayers. I also knew she had a daily walk with God, but it never dawned on me that her prayers were being answered when Willie passed. I often wondered why she could be so strong and courageous when his body was placed in the earth. I also noticed her carefree nature and free spirit when she returned home. She was given assurance that whether Willie lived or died, he would receive limited life in the physical world, but eternal life in the spiritual world. She waged in warfare with the angel of death, as well as with her own inhibitions and won victoriously over both. This is living proof that the Holy Spirit takes part in spiritual warfare.

My father told me some years later that the doctors said to him and my mother that there was nothing they could do for my brother. The cancer had destroyed every organ in his body. Whenever he received blood transfusions, it was like pouring water in a bucket with holes on all sides and the bottom. The blood transfusions were no help for his damaged organs.

Waging warfare is not always wrestling with the enemy or rebuking Satan. It is more akin to tearing down strongholds that are keeping us from understanding the real nature of the Holy Spirit and learning what it takes to move a living God. Before my mother could intercede on my brother's behalf, she had to release him to God and bind her own selfish desires to keep him alive. Releasing a child to the death angel is hard for any mother to do. This is proof that the Holy Spirit increases our faith to have complete trust in God during our times of sorrow and vulnerabilities.

SPIRITUAL WARFARE

My mother was no stranger to the pain and agony of losing a child. She lost an eight-year-old daughter to rabies in the early 40's. Carrie, my sister, was at recess while attending a school in the country. A rabid dog was seen in the area. The teacher could not round up all the children before the dog was on the school grounds. The children outside ran and locked themselves in an outside toilet. Carrie ran to the toilet and tried to get in, but the children were afraid to open the door. The dog jumped on her and tore her eye out of its socket.

Figure 22

Since there was no cure for rabies, the doctor suggested that my parents put her out of her misery. Carrie was buried in December while there was snow on the ground. For 35 years, my mother kept Carrie's green plaid dress and undershirt as a reminder of her life with the family. I never knew her, but she visited me one night in a dream. I woke up to find a tall woman leaning over me in a green plaid dress. I immediately knew it was her. She was warning me of the upcoming battle Satan would wage over my son and his battle with drugs.

When God came to take my mother home, I was in

Washington, DC at Arlington National Cemetery with my science students and my husband, Wendell. I was standing beside a tombstone when a large black bird came and perched on the headstone in front of me. Chills covered my arms and legs and my heart skipped a beat.

Figure 23

I immediately knew that this was a sign that something happened or was about to happen. I looked at my watch and it had stopped at 4:00 pm. I gathered all the students and went to the hotel. As soon as we got there, the manager ran to the bus and told me to call home immediately. Wendell called because I was too nervous and afraid to call. I knew that the message would be too unpleasant and dreadful for me to handle. I saw a sad look appear on his face. I spoke to my father and he told me my mother had a fatal heart attack at 4:00 pm. The ride back home was quiet and serene. I was crying inside but they were tears of joy because God had sent a sign at 4:00 pm to let me know exactly when He came to take my mother home. I was at peace with her death because God had sent a raven to let me know that her work on earth was finished. He sent me a token of flight to let me know that her spirit was alive. Just like the raven that perched on the tomb at Arlington National Cemetery got up and flew away, she too had taken her flight, so I rejoiced.

The Eight Weapons Used in Spiritual Warfare

There are six parts of the armor which are physical and two parts that require action on our part in order to set the physical parts of the armor in motion. The Holy Spirit tells us to stand still and watch God and His angels go to work on our behalf. They do all the fighting for us while we pray quietly in the spirit. These parts are listed below:

1. The helmet of salvation
2. The breastplate of righteousness
3. The belt of truth
4. The shield of faith
5. The sword of the Spirit (the Word of God)
6. The shoes of the gospel and peace
7. The tongue of prayer and supplication in the Spirit
8. The watchful eyes of perseverance and supplication for all believers

Having on the whole armor of God is an indication that we are spiritually trained by the Holy Spirit and are ready to take on the wiles of the devil. This armor, unlike military armor, is sealed within our minds, hearts, and souls. There is a halo of light all around us that only evil and Satan can see. We should never let this halo be removed by allowing ourselves to be deceived by the enemy. The suit of armor is not our armor, nor does it belong to any pastor, bishop, evangelist or any other spiritual leader. This armor is sealed on us by the Holy Spirit to protect us from the world, evil, principalities, and spiritual weaknesses in high places.

I often hear people say they are not strong, and they slip a lot because they have kinks in my armor. The kinks in the armor mindset are tricks of Satan to deceive you into believing that God's armor has no power.

The first step to remember is that we have no armor other than that which God gives. The Bible does not speak of my armor it specifically says to put on the whole armor of God. Any other armor is a false representation of the truth.

Satan does not want us to know how to defeat him and his evil cohorts. Never allow yourself to get caught up in his double talk when the Bible specifically tells us the truth. Remember Eve got caught up in the double talk of Satan when he tricked her into eating the forbidden fruit. Never put on this armor until you fully understand its design and purpose in God's plan of salvation.

Eve did not know she was the object of Satan's plan to destroy God's creation. She took what she received from Satan and shared it with Adam. Together, they received the knowledge of what Satan had spoken of, their eyes were opened. Satan took the word of God and twisted it to create doubt in Eve's mind. Eve made the decision to trust Satan and doubt the words of God.

That's how Satan tricks and deceives people. He creates doubt and people are then tempted to prove him right or wrong. Adam and Eve's rebellion released sin into the world and from that day were responsible for all their deeds and actions (**Genesis 3:1-7**).

Be careful what you ask for. Satan's deception caused them to be put out of the garden. It also brought sickness, physically challenging work and death upon them and the world. We were created to live in peace and pleasure forever. Playing around with Satan will cause you to lose or give up something valuable. I believe Eve's first child, Cain, was Satan's son. Jealously, hatred and murder rose in Cain and he killed his brother, Abel. Cain's life was spared, but he carried the mark of Satan with him. Satan ushered in evil, hatred, and murder through Cain's generation. Cain could never show faith or belief in God because he carried the genes of Satan.

God was not pleased with Cain's offering because God knew he was the offspring of Satan, and that is why Cain is not listed in the bloodline of Adam. The 42 generations of the birth of Christ omits Adam (**Matt. 1:1-17**). However, **Luke 3: 23-38**, traces the birth of Christ back to Adam but does not mention Cain or Abel. It ends with Adam's son Seth.

Since Satan's deception changed the course of humanity, God designed this spiritual armor for our protection so mankind will not be deceived by Satan again. It is our weapon against the evils that were loosed upon the earth. Notice, the warrior has the armor in areas to protect the body from the fiery darts, words of enticements, and trickery used by Satan and his cohorts. The head is covered with the helmet of salvation, so Satan cannot tamper with the mind as he confused Eve. The mind is where Satan sets up a battlefield to tempt, control and finally destroy. The breastplate covers the heart to protect the hidden treasures and living covenant God has written on the hearts of believers. If the devil can change our hearts from pure to unclean, we will never see God or our loved ones again. The loins are girded with the belt of truth for the strength needed to believe in our spiritual fight and to reject the words of Satan.

The shield is used as a symbol of faith in the belief that when Satan attacks from all angles, the body is safe. The arrows and darts of the enemy will be blocked by the shield, and any sickness brought on by Satan will not enter our bodies. The shoes protect the feet by walking peacefully with the gospel of Jesus as we encounter others, while the sword is the living Word of God, which is sharper than any two-edged cutting device. It can cut and divide the soul and spirit, bone and marrow, and discern the thoughts and intents of the heart. Prayer is an invisible weapon that the warrior uses to summons God and His angels. The watchful eyes let us know when evil is approaching so that God and His angels will be ready to attack, defeat and destroy our enemies. All we are required to do is pray and keep a watchful eye and stand and see the salvation of our God.

We cannot buy the armor, nor can we receive it from another warrior. We must walk and live the life and know that we are in God, He is in us and we are one with Him, in spirit and in truth. Once we are true believers, with an unyielding spirit that is rooted and grounded in faith and prayer, He issues His armor to us. Our wars are fought in the spiritual realm; they are not fought through flesh and blood. Therefore, we, in our physical bodies, can never enter this realm. Many often make the mistake of thinking they can use physical weapons to fight spiritual battles. Bringing worldly weapons to a spiritual fight gets us in a lot of trouble and prolongs situations that God and His angles could have easily taken care of. All we need to do is pray and have faith that God and His angels will do exactly what He said they would do.

The second step to remember is that God has given us the key to the door of His existence and power on earth. He wants us to carry on where Jesus left off. This key allows us to call forth His angels to fight our battles. Our faith tells us that if Christ said it, then it is already done. We need to get out of His way and let His angels remove the barriers in our lives.

The third step is that we must remember that this war is not against people. It is against demons, devils, and Satan who control people, situations, positions and the airways. Our prayers should not be against the people, but the demonic spirits that control them. That is the primary reason why our warfare is not effective. We are praying against flesh and blood when we should pray and command the demonic spirits that have taken over their bodies to come out and be silenced. When Jesus was casting out demons, He never carried on a conversation with them. He bound the demonic spirit first, cast him out and loosed blessings upon the victim.

My niece and I were discussing the condition of her mother,

and my oldest sister, Bunt, who was in a nursing home suffering from Alzheimer and dementia. She was listless, inactive, and lifeless. The family had contacted Hospice because her condition had worsened. We often said that these diseases were a result of Satan's chains of entrapment on the mind because she was listless, inactive and lifeless. We decided to lose Satan's hold on Bunt's mind and bind what Jesus refers to as the spirit of lunacy (lunatic), as recorded in Mark, chapter 5. We went to the nursing home to bind up the spirit of lunacy and loose the spirit of good health upon Bunt. My niece prayed silently while I read the scriptures and commanded this spirit to release my sister's mind and body. While we prayed and sang songs, we noticed that she was lifting her hands, praising God and talking with us. We were elated. We asked God to cover her in our absence. A few days later, we noticed a swollen mass beneath her neck that was causing her throat to close.

Hospice was scheduled to intervene because she was not responding to food or medicine. Several weeks passed and Hospice had not arrived. My niece decided to stop by, she noticed her mother's condition had worsened. She did not realize that when Hospice is called in, all other services stop. Since Hospice was not there, she called the ambulance services who took her mother to the local hospital. The hospital doctors were reluctant to diagnose the swelling under her neck because she was dehydrated and there were rules pending Hospice.

She called me and we started interceding and going into warfare. Soon after, her doctor quickly diagnosed her condition, ordered a feeding tube and told the family the mass beneath her neck needed to be surgically removed. He gave her antibiotics and scheduled surgery for three days later. We prayed for mercy and strength. The surgery went well, and the mass was an infected gland that needed draining. The coloration of Bunt's skin was radiant. She was smiling and talking with her children after the surgery. One of the nurses at the nursing home said the lady from Hospice had a wreck and that if she was at the nursing home when Bunt's condition worsened, Bunt would have died. Thank God for faith and prayer, and binding and loosing.

The fourth step to remember is that binding and loosing are important elements of warfare that must be taken seriously. We cannot have any openings or unrighteous relationships in our lives that are not sanctioned by God. We cannot have soft spots, such as sympathy or grief, for the possessed individual when we are at war with the enemy. The enemy sees all our faults as weaknesses and knows when we are not real.

Therefore, he will continue to possess the individual. Engaging in warfare with faults and undisclosed problems in our lives does harm to ourselves as well as the person we are trying to help. The fifth factor is if you have issues in your life that have not been resolved, correct them first before attempting to engage in warfare. The demons will crush you, once they see an opening.

The book of **Acts 19: 14-16** tell a story of Sceva, a Jewish priest, whose seven sons saw Paul cast demons out of a possessed young girl. They tried to imitate Paul, but the demon spoke to them and said, *"Jesus I know, and Paul I recognize, but who are you?"*

The evil spirit left the victim, jumped into the seven brothers, beat them and sent them into the streets naked and bleeding. Waging war in the spiritual realm is a serious matter we cannot take for granted. Just because we say we know Jesus does not give us the authority to engage in warfare. We must know the Father and His Holy Spirit and understand how each operates. We may have good intentions of just sitting in for spiritual support, but the evil spirits possessing a person will know if we are weak in our ability to drive the spirits out of the person who is possessed. We must be trained and equipped with the Word of God before we take on the task of casting out evil spirits. The scene below is the seven brothers casting out an evil spirit, but when the spirit came out, the brothers could not control it so it overtook them.

Figure 24

The Gospel of **John 14:12** (**KJV**) says, *"He that believeth on me, the works that I do shall he do also; and greater works than these he shall do; because I go unto my Father."* This is the doctrine upon which Jesus Christ spoke the world into existence through simple belief. When He said in **Genesis 1:3** (**KJV**), *"Let there be light,"* He was calling forth things from the spiritual realm that came into the natural realm as a solid form. He had already created in His mind what this form looked like. Therefore, He plucked it from His spiritual mind into natural existence and it became a real object.

We can do the same thing because **John 14:12** (**KJV**) says, *"Verily, verily, I say unto you, He that believeth on me, the works that I do shall he do also; greater works than these shall he do; because I go unto my Father."* Ministers have interpreted this verse to mean the greater works ceased when all the disciples died. I just do not believe this. This is what Satan wants us to believe. He wants to keep us in darkness so we will not know the mysteries, hidden codes, and symbols God has left for us in the Holy Scriptures.

There are many people, mostly women, across America who must meet in places other than the church to engage in spiritual warfare. They are reluctant to discuss spiritual warfare within the church for fear that those in authority will not approve of it or dismiss their actions as a disruptive process to dismantle church doctrines. There is very little information written or discussed on this topic because of its kinship to casting out demons, speaking in unknown tongues and speaking life into impossibilities. Most church administrators believe that if God did not give these gifts to the pastors of these churches, then they are not ordained by God. Many churches will not allow the laying on of hands to heal the sick but will participate in such activities for the ordination of deacons.

Possibly, their reluctance is because of their lack of understanding of the Holy Spirit and His role in spiritual warfare. When church leaders lack understanding of spiritual warfare, it causes a lack of understanding within their congregations as well. Knowing spiritual warfare helps us in many ways. I remember a situation at work where my enemies and some doubting parents wanted college professors who were chemistry and physic majors to sit in my classes to see if I knew my content. They tried everything to defeat me; even planting carcinogens in my room. Every attempt they made failed because the Holy Spirit warned me of their plans before they could put them in action.

They finally arranged for the area superintendent and the district science consultant to sit in and observe me as I taught. I had faith in God. I prayed a prayer of safety and protection to God and left the matter in His hands. I went to bed that night unaware that they would be there in the morning. The Holy Spirit laid me down to sleep that night with dreams that were comforting and reassuring that God was on the throne. While I was sleeping, the Lord sent a vision to calm my fears. I was in a circle with crosses surrounding me. There were angels descending and ascending from Heaven on a ladder. The descending angels had crosses in their hands and as they came down, they planted the crosses around me. Those who were ascending the ladder were going back to Heaven to get more crosses.

Figure 25

I knew this dream was real because God was showing me the same ladder He showed Jacob in his dream. The angels in Jacob's dream were also descending and ascending a ladder. **Genesis 28:12** says, *"He had a dream in which he saw a stairway resting on the earth, with its top reaching to heaven, and the angels of God were ascending and descending on it."* Then in **John 1:51**, it is written, *"Then He declared, "Truly, truly, I say to all of you that you will see heaven open and the angels of God ascending and descending on the Son of Man."* The Holy Spirit told me, "Fear not. I will cover you. This war is already won. While you remain asleep, my angels will fight this battle for and you will not have to lift a hand." I went to sleep that night, knowing that this battle was not my battle to fight. God has a wonderful way of letting us know that the wars we face in our earthly lives were never meant to be fought by us. He sends messengers to warn us, and angels to fight for us.

When I got to work, I was calm and rested. There were two adults in my room, the superintendent, and the science consultant. I spoke to them, ignored their routine observation and did my work as usual. They finally left after an hour. The science consultant walked toward the front of the room and placed a note on my desk. When the class was over, I read the personal note she left about my command of the course. She also left me a word of scripture from **Jeremiah 17:7-9**, which says, "B*lessed is the man who trusts in the Lord, whose hope is the Lord. He is like a tree planted beside waters that stretch out its roots to the stream. It fears not the heat when it comes, its leaves stay green. In the year of drought, it shows no distress, but still bears fruit.*" God had spoken to the heart of this woman who could see Christ in me. She understood the unyielding faith I had shown during this trial and how God had given me the victory. The matter was finally resolved.

There was another case when the Holy Spirit warned me of things to come. When my youngest daughter, Crystal, was at the Medical University of South Carolina (MUSC) awaiting surgery, I was quickly moved to pray in the spirit for her life. When I got home from school, I received a call from my sister who stayed with my daughter during the week. Although my sister has grown children of her own, she has been like a second mother to my children. She said the doctor could not operate or move Crystal because fever had invaded her body. I finished all my activities at home, checked on my other daughter, Angela, who was a senior in college and my son Wendell, a sophomore in high school. I fixed my husband's supper and went into an empty room to engage in warfare. I began to pray. I saw spirits of infirmities enter my daughter's body. They were transparent, but I could see their outlines. They stretched themselves to fit over her body, pulling, tucking and squeezing themselves just like a plastic glove adheres to a person's hands. They were embedded within her and no one could see them, not even her caregivers. They just absorbed themselves into her body and took possession of her body and mind.

They manifested themselves in the form of a high fever and spoke in her voice as if she was in a state of derision. Her body was not responding to the medication that the doctors were giving for her. The spirits of infirmities were in control. Just as they were causing her temperature to spike well above 103 degrees, I saw Jesus enter the room and lay down inside of her body to cover her from the damage the spirits of infirmities were causing in her body. The Bible states in **Matt.8:17**, *"This was to fulfill what was spoken through Isaiah the prophet: HE HIMSELF TOOK OUR INFIRMITIES AND CARRIED AWAY OUR DISEASES."*

Figure 26

The doctor discussed an x-ray with us that showed sacs of pus and blockages in her intestine, and she needed surgery to remove all the scar tissue. They also said that her veins were scarce, and they could not guarantee her full recovery. She was a very sick child. Wendell and I prayed, and I called my prayer partner, who was a devout prayer warrior. God answered our prayers and Crystal did not need the surgery. As my prayer partner would say of God, "I can't doubt Him because I know too much about Him."

Crystal remained in remission for five years. During those years, she got married, but her doctor said she would never have any children. Then one day as I was coming home from school, God showed me an open vision of a baby boy with green eyes and brown hair. Our first grandson, Desean, was born the following year in March. Crystal's health remained good during her pregnancy, but eventually, several months after the baby was born, her intestines flared up again and she had to be hospitalized.

The doctor showed us an x-ray of her intestines matted together and said, "This is just like cement. I do not know how we are going to operate or correct this condition; it is beyond anything we can do here." The doctor said they wanted her to go to Emory Medical Hospital for surgery. I began to pray as I was driving home from work the following day. I do not remember seeing any cars on the road when God showed me an open vision of Crystal in her hospital bed. She was weeping in pain and quietly calling Jesus' name.

The Holy Spirit showed me Jesus walking down the halls of the hospital. The halls were crowded with nurses and doctors dispensing medicine to the patients. There were doctors going in and out of patients rooms. Visitors were lining the walls of the halls waiting to see their family members. I saw Jesus walk pass them knowing exactly where He was going. No one saw Him or heard Him walking in the halls. They had no idea that He was in the building. Everyone continued to carry out their daily duties. Then He walked to Crystal's door, walked through the door and over to her bedside. Crystal was not aware that He was there. She continued to call His name until she quickly fell asleep. My fears began to vanish because I knew He had heard my prayer and had come to see about my child. I felt my heart leap for joy that Jesus took time from His busy work to hear my prayers and the cries of my child. I felt so humbled and blessed that of all the people in the hospital, He chose to stop by my child's room on His journey to heal the sick and ease their pain.

Figure 28

He put His right hand into her stomach, twisted His arm back and forth, removed it and quickly disappeared. He was showing me that I had no reasons to worry because He had already corrected the problem. I told Crystal what I saw. A glow came across her face. She said, "Then I will not have to wear a colostomy bag." I held her in my arms and said, "No, Chris you will not wear a colostomy bag." She was encouraged as we drove to Emory Medical Center. The surgery was scheduled for the following day, but she developed a fever during the night. Her fever was so high and the spirits of infirmities had returned. They started using Chris' voice and began calling me all kind of obscene names. They said I was nobody and did not deserve a husband like her father. If God had not prepared me already to deal with these spirits, I would have spoken out in anger to my daughter. Instead, I began a silent prayer that intensified into warfare and speaking in an unknown tongue until the voices stopped. I left the room, went to the gift shop, bought a red rose and a scriptural reading of the 23rd Psalm.

Figure 29

I laid the red rose (a symbol of love) on her stomach and read **Psalm 23** aloud. Then I began to go into warfare and prayed with such intensity that I was speaking in tongues. The spirits of infirmities left her body and she started crying asking for forgiveness for what she believed the spirit of infirmities had done. The nurse came in, took her temperature and it was normal. They immediately began prepping for surgery which would take place three hours later.

The team of doctors came in to speak to us. The head doctor referred to the x-rays that were sent to them from my home hospital and said that the ones they took showed the same thing. They said, "With her intestine so tangled and matted, they would have to remove the majority of her intestines and place a colostomy bag on her side." Chris rose up and said, "My mother said I would not need a colostomy bag. She said, 'God had fixed everything." The doctor looked at me in disbelief. I told him that our faith in God was strong and I believed that God would produce a miracle. He said that the x-rays showed something different and we need to be realistic. I told my daughter to release her fears as they carried her to surgery. God would do exactly what He showed me. I told her to have faith in what God had shown me instead of what the doctors were saying. Gods' words do not come back void.

I went outside along with nine months old Desean, pushing him in a baby carriage, while my husband stayed in the waiting room. I walked the grounds with an assurance that God was going to fix everything. I had a spirit of confirmation and truth that no one could shake. I just believed that God was going to do exactly what He said He would do. Negative thoughts about what the doctor had said tried to enter my mind, but I closed them out and would not allow them to weigh me down.

I pushed my grandson around the university grounds for several hours, smiling and humming a song of praise and worship so that evil thoughts would not enter my mind. I thanked God and His Holy Spirit for the freedom from worry and insecurities. God was a leaning post that kept me standing and a rock that shielded me from hurt and pain. I felt honored that He was keeping me from the evil thoughts of the enemy.

I decided to go in and check on my husband and assure him that God was in the midst. I was pushing Desean down the hall when I saw the doctor running toward me saying, "There must be a God somewhere because when we opened her up and looked inside, I could take my fingers and move them in and between her intestines with ease. They moved freely and the matted cement structures we saw on the X-rays were gone!" He was so excited and overjoyed because he didn't have to remove a large portion of her intestines after all.

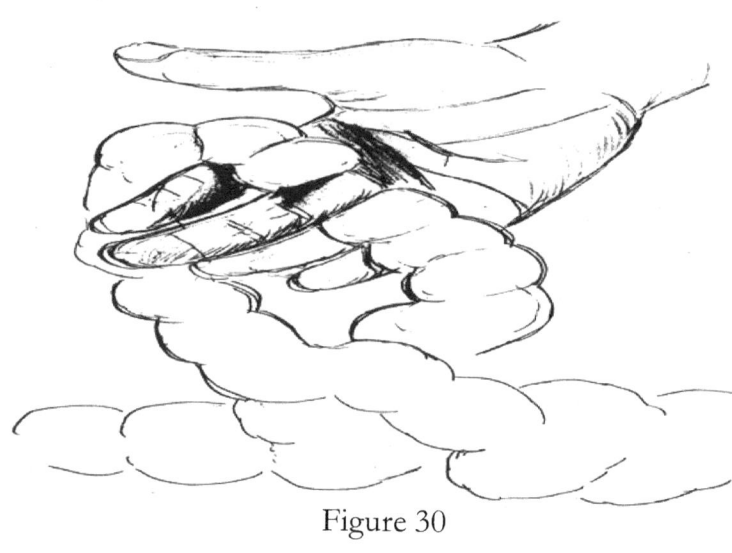

Figure 30

He said, "We only had to remove a few centimeters of her intestines and sewed her up." My mind quickly went to the vision of Jesus reaching down in my daughter's stomach and twisting His arm back and forth. The doctor was doing the same thing with his hands. God fought this battle several days ago and gave us the victory. These examples were warfare at its highest level. The rudiments of warfare are not learned overnight and it should not be taken lightly. There are several scriptural references we must learn before we began warfare. Satan knows that beginners in warfare are hampered by lack of scriptural knowledge. He uses this weakness as a tool to ward off warriors to prevent them from attacking him. Satan knows that we cannot banish nor cast him into outer darkness as we can do with demons or evil spirits.

The thing we can do is cover ourselves in the words of Jesus and spit them at Satan when he confronts us. We must read and be able to recite certain scriptures from memory. The only weapon we have against him is the power to rebuke and reprove with scriptures using the name of Jesus. Resisting the devil with the name Jesus causes him to flee, but it will not keep him away forever. A steadfast life of faith and prayer alone with the name of Jesus will cause him to stay a distance from us, but he will forever remain in the background, waiting for an opening or for us to make an error. Use these primary verses when confronted by Satan:

1. *"I destroy any arguments and every pretension that sets itself up against the knowledge of God, and I take captive every thought to make it obedient to Christ."* **2 Cor. 10:5**

2. *"I am from God and have overcome them. Greater is He who is in me than he who is in the world."* **1 John 4:4**

3. *"No weapon formed against me shall prosper and every tongue that accuses me in judgment, I will condemn."* **Isaiah 54:17**

Once you decide to become a true warrior, fighting the good fight, these evil forces will follow you wherever you go. The key to keeping evil away and enjoying peace and harmony is to live a life of faith and prayer and believing in the impossible. We must also believe that God can, and will do all things but fail. We must truly believe that He is our Great I Am. He says so in the following scriptures:

"I am the Door"	**John 10:9-16**
"I am the Living Bread"	**John 6:51**
"I am the Light of the World"	**John 9:5**
"I am the Good Shepherd"	**John 19:11**
"I am the Resurrection and the Life"	**John 11:25**
"I am the Son of God"	**Matthew 27:43**
"I am the Way, the Truth and the Life"	**John 14:6**
"I am the True Vine"	**John 15:1**
"I am Jesus..."	**Acts 26:15**
"I am the God of your fathers"	**Acts 7:32**
"I am who I am"	**Exodus 3:14**

HOW TO RELEASE THE POWER OF SPIRITUAL WARFARE
Chapter 5

Increasing faith has been a personal desire of believers since the disciples asked Jesus to increase their faith over two thousand years ago. Many people, even believers who waver in their belief, want increased faith. However, because they are not willing to wait for the increase, they go about their lives lacking faith and power to call things into existence. Faith is like a precious jewel, it is priceless. However, when faith is lost it can be difficult to find. Increased faith gives the believer a holy boldness and courage to face tumultuous plights in their daily Christian walk.

Even the disciples of Jesus Christ needed an increase in their faith. They had the author and finisher of faith in their midst to serve as their mentor and set examples for them. Jesus Christ was the seed spoken of in **Gal 3: 16**. Therefore, faith, one of the fruits of the Spirit as well as one of the gifts of the Holy Spirit, was the essence of what the disciples were asking Jesus for. No doubt, they probably, at this stage in their development as believers, knew very little about the Holy Spirit and His embodiment in Jesus Christ. They were knowledgeable enough to know that Jesus was unlike any other man they had encountered, but they did not truly know who He was.

They were present when Jesus spoke to the devil in Luke 8:30, and cast 3,000 – 6,000 demons out of the man living in the cemetery. It was not unusual during those days, to see people who practiced the occult and many proselytes cast out demons. They were present when Jesus said in **Luke 8:45-46**, *"Who touched me?"*

SPIRITUAL WARFARE

The disciples said it must have been someone in the crowd; to them was also not unusual. Jesus, more adamantly said, "Somebody has touched me: for I perceive that virtue (healing) is gone out of me."

Figure   31

    A woman, with an issue of blood for twelve long years, spoke up and told Him she had touched the hem of His garment and her issue of blood was quickly sealed up. Jesus looked at her and told her that her healing was a result of exercising her faith (bearing her fruit). Then He gave her another fruit of the Holy Spirit when He told her to go in peace. This is the point when the disciples began to realize the magnitude of His power. They had witnessed the miracle of healings; the healing of the man with palsy; the man with the withered hand; and they heard Him speak life to the Centurion's servant. They had witnessed Him restoring life to the son of the widow of Nain, rebuking the wind and calming the raging waters, feeding the 5,000, forgiving the sins of the woman with the Alabaster box, and speaking with power and authority. Yet, despite all of the faith and fruit-bearing exercises they had witnessed, something was different about this healing. Imagine the disciples saying, "How could He distinguish one touch from all of the others in this large crowd of people?" Imagine the disciple, John, saying, "But He said He felt virtue (healing) leaving His body." Now, imagine them looking at each other as if a light came on in each of their heads. They saw that Jesus did not say a word to the woman or even touch her as He had done with the other miracles. They heard Him say that goodness and healing had left His body. Jesus feels our pain and sickness the same way. Our faith, like this woman's, is what heals us. There are no boundaries that can hold or contain faith. That is why faith is a gift and a fruit of the Holy Spirit.

The disciples knew, without a doubt, that there was something that set Him apart from ordinary men. That something was the fruits and gifts of the Holy Spirit. They had just seen the works of the Holy Spirit manifested through the body of Jesus, but had no idea what role the Holy Spirit would play in their lives. Then Jesus Christ, in **Luke 17**, spoke to them about offenses such as resentment, indignation, insults, and disrespect.

When Jesus spoke about forgiving others seventy times seven and asking for repentance, the disciples were even more baffled. The disciples saw that they needed something extra within their bodies that would calm them and allow them to be like Jesus. They really wanted the same virtue they saw operating in Jesus. They said in **Luke 17:5**, *"Lord, increase our faith."* Later in **Luke 17:6**, Jesus explained how they could move a tree with faith the size of a mustard seed.

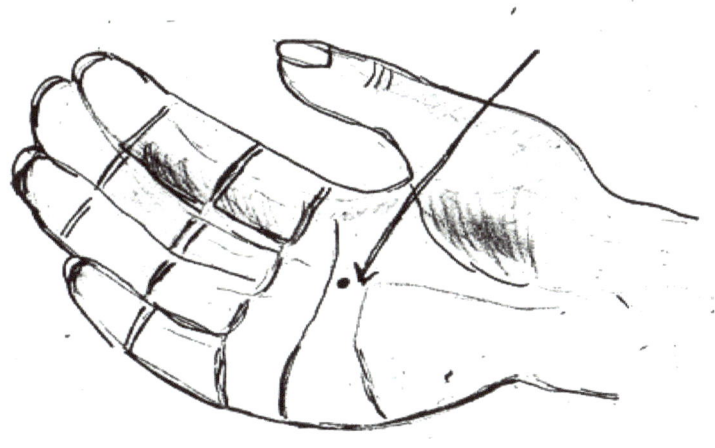

Figure 32

The mustard seed is a very small seed that can be easily lost because of its size. Once the seed is placed in the ground, its limbs and boughs grow as any tree in the forest. Birds and other fowls of the air make their homes and nest in the leaves of their limbs. This kind of faith must be practiced for spiritual warfare. Jesus knew the disciples were not ready to receive this gift without a knowledge of the Holy Spirit, so He gave them conditions and examples by saying, *"If your faith was as small as a mustard seed, you might say unto this sycamore tree, be thou plucked up by the root and be thou planted in the sea, and it should obey you."* **Luke 17:6**. The use of the words if, might, and should, indicates that Jesus knew the disciples were not ready to handle such power and authority. Jesus knew that their greatest trials were yet to come.

Believe in the Impossible

One of the basic problems with spiritual warfare is that many people refuse to believe in the impossible. If it did not happen to them, they refuse to believe that it can happen to anyone else. They fail to realize that God recognizes and takes care of His own.

People are quick to believe that God gives them the desires of their hearts, but fail to delight themselves in Him as the Scriptures require. My prayer partner, a 103-year-old minister who died several years ago, had a profound faith in God and believed that God could do anything. She never questioned anyone's faith or their walk with God. She would just say, "If they are not right, they will find themselves on a sliding board to Hell." We agreed that whoever died first would find a way to let the other know that they made it in. The first night of her death, I had a vision of a train with saints on their way to heaven. She was on that train and stood up and waved her hand to let me know she made it in.

Figure 33

When Christians face hard tasks in life, they must have made-up minds that no matter what happens, they will not turn back or quit. Developing increasing faith can be a hard task, but remember, you want to increase your faith in God. If you are not ready to make this giant step in your life, it is best to approach it gradually rather than going cold turkey doing it all at once. It works for some when they are truly determined and have a thirst for the increase. If you are truly serious about the increase, you will find that you will not have to stop any habits such as smoking, drinking, cheating, slippery tongue or other undesirable traits. God can take all the undesirables away in an instant. When you realize it, they are all gone and never to return.

That's the kind of God we serve. The following scriptures validate the power of faith.

> *"Now unto Him, that can do exceeding abundantly above all that we ask or think, according to the power that works in us."*
> **Ephesians 3:20**

"Without faith, it is impossible to please him." **Hebrews 11:6**

No matter how good we are and how many times we attend church, give to the poor, tithe, or offer our bodies as sacrifices, without faith, we will never please God. We can sing the songs of Zion that cause tears to fall from worshippers eyes, we can quote scriptures every minute of the day or preach a sermon where the entire church comes to the altar, but without faith, we cannot please God. How can we believe in the impossible? Believing the impossible begins with allowing God to purge us. Purging is allowing Him to remove all the impurities from our lives. You will never be able to remove those things or clean up your life on your own. Purging hurts because you are losing something that has been a part of you for a long time, but do not fret because it will be a blessing and there will be no scars.

Believe everything God said in the scriptures, even if it sounds impossible. Be eager to receive the teachings and messages coming from the Holy Spirit. Trust, lean and depend on God for your being and your existence. Trust the Holy Spirit. Believe that He does speak to you and you hear Him. If you are not sure, try the spirit by the spirit to see if it is of God. In other words, something is wrong if you are thinking about an apple and the word you hear is an orange. The devil cannot read our minds, but, the Holy Spirit can.

Read the Bible and Quote Powerful Scriptures

Timothy says in **2 Timothy 2:5 (KJV)**, *"Study to show thyself approved unto God, a workman that need not to be ashamed rightly dividing the word of truth."* The Word of God, when studied under the guidance of the Holy Spirit, gives the believer a boldness to speak in truth and not be fearful. The Word says, *"For God has not given us a spirit of fear; but of power, and of love and of a sound mind,"* **2 Tim.1-7(NKJV)**. *"Iron sharpens iron, so a man sharpens the countenance of his friend,"* **Proverbs 27:17 (KJV)**. In other words, to know more about Jesus read His word. If you want your friend to walk in faith, tell him/her to read the Bible so that the two of you will learn from each other and agree on the Word of God.

Reading the Bible keeps us closer to God. It keeps us focused on the will of God and His purpose for our lives. The acronym for B.I.B.L.E. is Basic Instructions Before Leaving Earth. Understand that it is the roadmap with directions on how to please God on Earth and continue with Him in the Heavens. It gives us strength in the times of weakness, courage when our hearts fail us, and it gives us the power to rebuke Satan and reprove our enemies.

There are scriptures that bring about healing. When reading the healing scriptures, insert your name in the place of the person in the verses. Deliverance and salvation scriptures work the same way. The reason the Word produces healings, miracles, and prophecies is because the Bible is the living Word. The Bible is the Word of God. The Bible speaks to us through the Holy Spirit, who is a teacher, counselor, comforter and brings things to our remembrance.

Satan has devised a method of hiding the Word of God from

man by placing deceptive and distractive thoughts in his mind that the Bible is dull and not interesting to read. Many people living in a contemporary age believe that the Bible is a book of fantasies and the miracles of healings, and deliveries from the bondage of sin never took place. These people are members of the world of sight. They, like doubting Thomas, must see Him to believe Him. They, like the virgins with no oil in their lamps, must be prepared to receive Him.

Satan does not want our eyes to be open. He knows that once we can see spiritually, he has lost his hold and influence over you. His flirtatious moves and cunning tricks have no effect upon the believer. When our minds are occupied with the Holy Spirit, there is no opening for Satan to slip through.

I realized, during my teen years, that Satan had blinded me. He knew that my pact with God would separate me from God and that was what he wanted, spiritual death. I have thanked God many times over and over that He never took His hands off me. God saw beyond the veil whereas Satan cannot see into the future. He sees in the present time frame. That is why he must constantly steal, deceive and destroy believers in Christ. I really had to work hard at increasing my faith.

Figure 34

I went to college three years after making the pact with God. As I unpacked I found a Bible neatly tucked under my clothes.

When I went to bed at night, I would dream about the verses God wanted me to read. I constantly saw Psalm 6. I knew that God was grooming me, but the final part of the psalm gave me peace because the ninth verse says, "the Lord has heard my plea and will receive my prayers."

Develop a Godly Prayer Life

Prayer is communication with God. When we pray, we should pray to God and not to the Holy Spirit. We pray to the Father, in the name of Jesus, and in the presence of the Holy Spirit. Paul says in **Romans 8:26-27 (NIV)**, *"In the same way, the Spirit helps us in our weakness. We do not know what we ought to pray for, but the Spirit himself intercedes for us with groans that words cannot express. And He who searches our hearts knows the mind of the Spirit, because the Spirit intercedes for the saints in accordance with God's will."* Pray for results.

Figure 35

Interceding is a wonderful work of the Holy Spirit. Just as the Holy Spirit intercedes for us on earth, Jesus intercedes for us in heaven and stands in the gap between us and the Father, and speaks on our behalf. There are several reasons why Jesus told His disciples He had to leave them. He said if He did not leave, the Holy Spirit could not become known to man and live on earth within him. Interceding for us is only one of the many tasks performed by Jesus Christ. The Spirit of Jesus is seen on earth by many believers and converts as He and the Holy Spirit move in and out of the realms of the Earth and Heaven. There are times when we have problems knowing what to say to God, but in those times the Holy Spirit takes over our thoughts and minds and speaks to God for us. He knows exactly what we want to say and how we want to talk to God. When we see and hear people rocking and moaning as they pray, the Holy Spirit is interceding for them. Some even start speaking in tongues, which is a prayer language understood by the Holy Spirit. They have no idea what they are saying but they feel relieved and refreshed when they rise from their prayers. They are aware that the Holy Spirit was controlling them.

Never doubt your Faith

Believe in what you are doing. Do not be uncertain or have misgivings about your faith. Develop the innocent, child-like belief you had on Christmas Eve when you knew something special was under the tree for you. Godly faith is like throwing all your hang-ups, bad habits and self-consciousness away, and taking on a child's beliefs. God can deal with us when we are real. Believing is a test of faith, but all things are possible through the eyes of a child. Believe, knowing that your prayers are already answered.

Children are innocent, have pure hearts, and are quick to believe. They need no proof, no test of reliability or credibility to believe in Jesus, Santa Claus, the Easter bunny or even the Boogie Man. These beings have been rooted and grounded in their cultures. They have no reservations in believing that these beings really exist. As children grow older, they are told that these individuals are not real, but are make-believe characters.

Somehow, Jesus is thrown in with the other characters and has become a fairy tale in the minds of teens, adolescents, and even adults. Thus, more people are growing up without a solid relationship that is rooted and grounded in Jesus Christ. They have no clue of His power, saving grace or redemptive nature. Many people have become victims of social media where you touch and feel the wave while you are drawn into a world of make-believe and instant success. Satan has managed to elude himself of this world of fantasy and is more real in the mind of people than Jesus Christ. Satan, whether we call him the devil, Lucifer, angel of darkness, or the dragon, is familiar in the minds of more people than the name of Jesus. More people, young and old, are tossed into this realm of darkness because they have been convinced that there is power in following and worshiping Satan.

We as Christians must never forget that Satan has no more power than God allows him to have. He must ask permission from God before he can test a believer. This is clear in **Job 1:12**, *"And the LORD said unto Satan, Behold, all that he (Job) hath is in thy power; only upon him put not forth thine hand. So, Satan went forth from the presence of the LORD."* Remember, Satan has no more power than God allows him to have.

Satan has been using evil tactics since the beginning of time to get even with God since Michael, the archangel, kicked him out of Heaven **Rev.12:7-12 (KJV)**. Since Satan was an archangel, (Lucifer), he has a right to appear before God as the other angels, and make requests **Job 1:6**. His requests are of an evil nature. God grants Satan permission to test us in the hope that we will not fail, but if we are weak, God always provides a way of escape for the

SPIRITUAL WARFARE

believer, **1 Corinthians 10:13**.

Though Satan tempts us, Jesus is right there praying for us. This is clear in **Luke 22:32** when Jesus told Peter: "*...But I have prayed for your strength and endurance.*" It is a wonderful thing to know that Jesus has already prayed for us before the battles begin. Therefore, our fretting and stressing is all for naught. We have the victory. We must remain faithful through our trials and tribulations. Having someone to pray for you is very important. My prayer partner and I prayed together for years. We held hands. While she prayed, the Holy Spirit showed me all things that would come to pass, present and in the future.

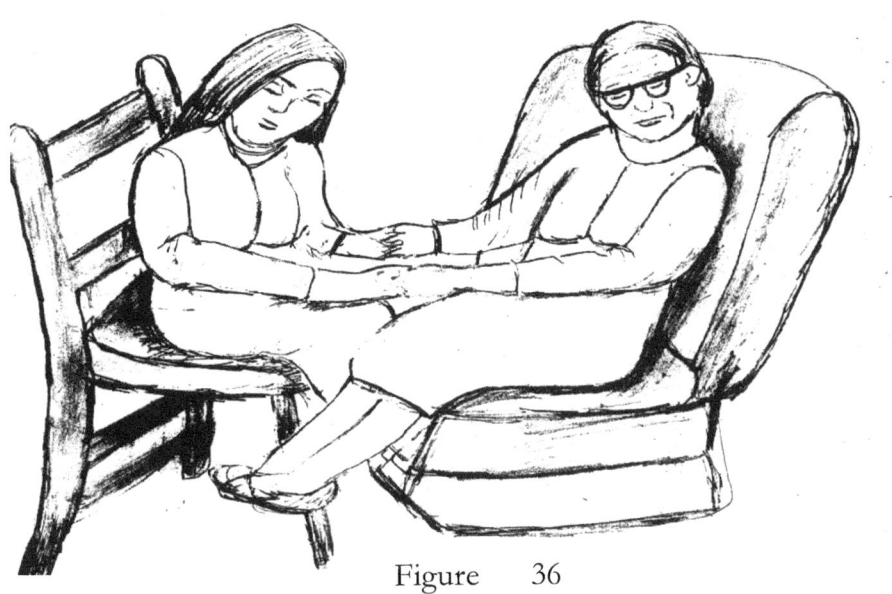

Figure 36

I saw my own family and my prayer partner's family prosper in health and wealth. I saw the memberships of my church family grow. I saw healing, financial and social seeds that I planted, grow up and blossom. I saw houses and cars, land, and wealth come into my possession. I saw the rise and fall of world leaders, religious leaders, and many more things. I never doubted anything the Holy Spirit showed me. My faith was strong, and my prayer life was full of bliss. I practiced what my prayer partner always said, "I can't doubt Him because I know too much about Him."

When you have faith, boldness, confidence and a constant prayer life, whatever the problem, God will fix it. You must go through the test to determine the grade. Every time we fail a test, Satan gets the credit. The closer we are to God, the less fear and doubt we will have. Praying to Him will become as natural as talking to a friend. What better friend to have than Jesus?

Pray Without Ceasing

Never stop praying. This is exemplified in **1 Thessalonians 5:17 (KJV)**. There are several scriptures which discuss the importance of prayer. **Matthew 21:22** says, *"And whatsoever you ask in prayer, you will receive, if you have faith."* Notice, the key provision and condition referenced, "if you have faith." Praying without faith brings no results. That is one of the reasons why so many people become angry and disappointed with God. They have no faith when they pray, and then they pray one or two times and stop. You must continue to pray, even if you think you are praying too much. God loves persistent people who never give up. We should pray and not lose heart. **Luke 18:2-5** says, *"There was in a city a judge, which feared not God, neither regarded man: And there was a widow in that city; and she came unto him, saying, avenge me of mine adversary and he would not for a while: but afterward he said within himself, Though I fear not God, nor regard man; Yet because this widow troubles me, I will avenge her, lest by her continual coming she weary me."*

When we are persistent in our prayers, God is quick to respond. Our persistence tells Him that we are in dire need and we know of no other God who can do these things. God loves to hear us call His name. It lets Him know that we place Him above all other powers and that He is omnipotent, omnipresent and omniscient.

When we are persistent, it lets Him know that we believe in Him and have faith that He will do just what He said He would do. Paul says **Gal. 6:9**, *"And let us not be weary in well doing: for in due season we shall reap, if we faint not."* God is true and faithful to His promises. He promised to be with us unto the end of the earth.

I remember my mother teaching us how to pray. She opened the Bible to **Matt. 6: 9-15**, and showed us the model prayer that Jesus taught His disciples. She explained every verse to us. Then she said, "You do not have to pray like this, but let God know your heart and what you are praying for. He loves to hear us praise Him. The more we praise Him, more blessings He will place upon us," she added.

Below are five powerful reasons for prayer:

1. It puts us in direct contact with God. The Bible says in **1 John 5:14 (NIV)**, *"This is the confidence we have in approaching God: that if we ask anything according to His will, He hears us."*

2. It allows us to see into the future. God said in **Jeremiah 33:3 (NIV)**, *"Call to me and I will answer you and tell you great and unsearchable things you do not know."*

3. It gives us confidence. **Hebrews 4:16 (NIV)** says, *"Let us then approach God's throne of grace with confidence, so that we may receive mercy and find grace to help us in our time of need."*

4. Prayer is powerful because it lets us know our cries go directly to Him.

5. Prayer causes us to worship and praise God even though we may be in prison. Luke writes in **Acts 1: 14 (NIV)**, *"About midnight Paul and Silas were praying and singing hymns to God, and the other*

prisoners were listening to them." God opened the prison doors for Paul and Silas.

Yes, prayer is powerful because when we add it to our faith, God will move mountains and any obstacles in our path and will quickly come to our rescue.

THE SHEKINAH GLORY EXPERIENCE
Chapter 6

$\mathcal{E}$ntering God's presence and the Shekinah Glory experience is where we feel love, grace, and mercy through the Father, Son, and Holy Spirit at the same time. Every believer does not have this encounter, but those who do will never forget it. I experienced this presence 10 years ago when I was taken up into the Holy of Holies; into the presence of God. The place was so bright that I could hardly see. I felt a warm feeling fall over my body like I'd never felt before. I saw figures gathered in the room, but because of the intensity of the white light and white cloud, I could not distinguish who they were. I forced myself to look, despite the bright glare that was hurting my eyes. I saw outlines of people in robes standing in a circle, and a tall large figure standing in the center. He had the face of a lamb and horns curved around His ears.

Figure 37

When he realized that I had seen him, he locked his eyes on my eyes. His eyes were searching and filled with unconditional love. I felt such a warm glow with feelings of peace and deep love. Then, I felt strong intense light piercing my body. I looked down and saw rays of light flowing from all parts of my body: my hands, arms, legs, feet, stomach, chest, mouth, eyes, nose and every inch of my body.

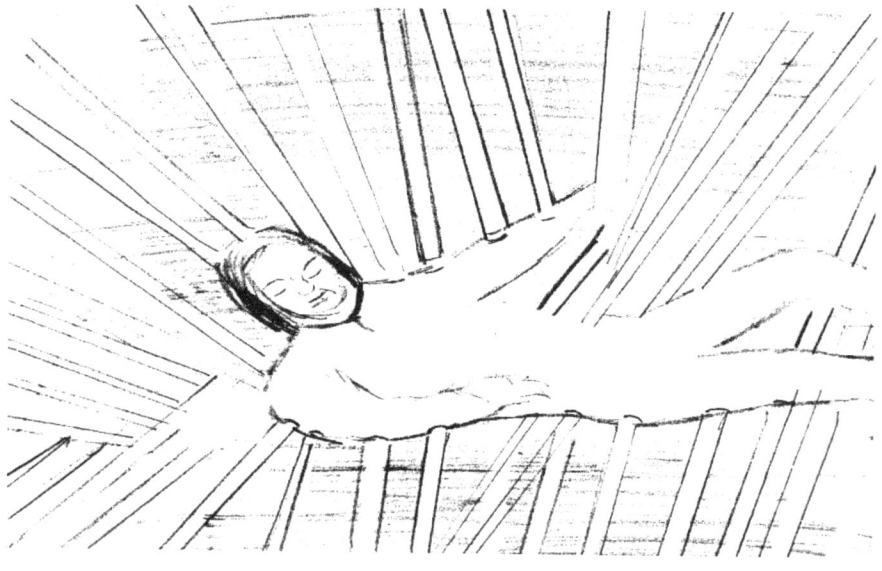

Figure 38

I also noticed that I was suspended in mid- air with no forms of attachments clinging to my body. I later found reference to this experience in **Habakkuk 3:4** which says, *"His radiance is like the sunlight; He has rays flashing from His hand, and there is the hiding of His power."*

I felt light-weighted and super-alive as if I was transformed into another body. I was floating through the darkness with the glory light emanating from every punctured place in my body. I was one with the Trinity in mind body and Spirit. The glow and the feelings of eternal peace and everlasting love remain with me: even to this day. I have never been the same since that encounter. I often have flashbacks of the moment when his searching eyes pierced my eyes and looked deep within my soul and filled me with his Shekinah glory.

Since then, I have felt someone's presence __ walking with me and sitting on the bed beside me at night. I even feel as if someone is watching over me and keeping evil spirits from entering my body. I often see pockets of blue light, which is an intense form of white light flashing in my bedroom at night fall. It comes very close to me that I have even reached out in the dark to touch it. I see an electric arc and feel a slight electrical shock. I am not frightened by it, nor am I afraid to sleep when it is near. I only know that it brings me peace and a sense of belonging to know that I am not alone.

The ultimate stage of spiritual warfare is getting to the place where you can walk in God's Shekinah Glory as well as enter his presence at will. The Shekinah Glory is a place in God where his power is so bright and awesome that it is virtually impossible to see your surroundings. The glow from his presence is blinding. This is white light at its highest level of intensity. This light has a drawing effect that captivates the mind, body and soul. It has an overwhelming effect that can cause a person to go into a trance or elevate to a level in Christ where only a few have been able to attain.

According to Webster's Revised Unabridged Dictionary (1913), shaken, (Shekinah), which means to inhabit, is a word taken from the Hebrew Talmud. "Shekinah refers to the visible majesty of the Divine Presence, especially when resting or dwelling between the cherubim on the mercy seat, in the Tabernacle, or in the Temple of Solomon; a term used in the Targum and by the later Jews, and adopted by Christians" (p.1327).

This word is not recorded directly in the Bible, but there are several references to it in the Old and New Testaments. Shekinah is referred to in the Bible as "Fire from heaven" "The Glory Cloud." and "God's Glory." According to The Strongest Strong's Exhaustive Concordance of the Bible (2001), the word fire ("God's glory") is mentioned more than 600 times: denote the word fire, number 784.

David Wilkerson (1999) writes, "No man can rightly define glory, any more than he can define God. Glory is the fullness of God, and that is a subject too high for our finite minds. Yet, we do know in part. When God gives His glory, He gives Himself. He cannot parcel Himself out in pieces - no man receives a portion, but all."

The Glory of God is introduced in the Bible in the book of Exodus when Moses saw a bush burning in the desert. The book of **Exodus 3:2 (KJV)** says, *"And the angel of the LORD appeared unto him in a flame of fire out of the midst of a bush: and he looked, and, beheld, the bush burned with fire, and the bush was not consumed."* The bush burned with an intense flame, but the leaves were not scorched nor were they completely burned to ashes.

The Old Testament records fire coming down from heaven in the following scriptures: a pillar of fire on Sinai (**Ex.19:18**), fire in the flame on the altar (**Judg. 13:20**), and God answering by fire (**1 Kings 18:24, 38**). Moses and the Israelites saw the pillar of fire and the pillar of cloud leading them out of Egypt. *"And the LORD went before them by day in a pillar of cloud to lead them along the way, and by night in a pillar of fire to give them light, that they might travel by day and by night. The pillar of cloud by day and the pillar of fire by night did not depart from before the people"* **Ex. 13:21-22 (ESV)**.

According to the Exodus 14, (**NKJV**), the Israelites were being pursued by the Egyptians as they were crossing the Red Sea. The Israelites panicked when they saw the Egyptians gaining on them. Then Moses spoke the courageous words often preached by passionate preachers: *"Stand still and see the salvation of the Lord"*

(**Exodus 14:13**). The angel of the Lord and the pillar of cloud that were in front of the Israelites went behind them and stood between them and the Egyptians. The pillar of cloud was darkness for the Egyptians, but daylight continued for the Israelites until they were on the other side of the Red Sea. Then, the Egyptian saw God's glory as he spoke to them from the pillar of fire and cloud. They were terrified because when they heard the voice in the cloud and saw God's face in the cloud.

This is the image of God that was revealed to me. This image is based on **Rev.1:13-15**. I heard him speak and beheld his glory. His entire face was on fire, even his hair, eyes, eyebrow and mouth. I was not frightened nor feared death. I was in a hypnotic state similar to a trance.

Figure 39

The Egyptians saw their death at hand. Getting to the Israelites and destroying them quickly vanished from their minds. God had said no man shall see His face and live. I believe this statement referred to non-believers only. Moses saw Him several times and lived.

The Egyptians tried to turn around and go back, but their wheels were removed by the Lord as they struggled to drive their chariots on the seabed. In their haste to get away, they said, *"Let us flee from the face of Israel for the Lord fight for them against the Egyptians,"* **Ex.14:25**. Then Moses was told by the Lord to stretch out His hand over the sea and the wall of water fell upon the Egyptians and drowned them. When we consider all the plagues that came upon the Egyptians, the death of their firstborn and the massive show of grief and pain they encountered, we see that these catastrophes did not move the Egyptians. It was only when they saw the glory of the Lord, did they realize that God had fused the faith of Moses with the constant prayers of the Israelites. They saw, through God's wrath and vengeance, the evidence and substance of God's power as the fire from His Shekinah Glory was about to descend upon them.

As strange as it may appear, this power brings release, cleansing, sustained faith and freedom of oppression. Jesus said in **Matt. 13:43**, *"The righteous shall shine forth as the sun."* He also said to the woman in **John 11:40** *"Did I not say to you that if you believe, you will see the glory of God?"* I truly believe that is why I have been blessed like the woman in the book of John because I BELIEVE!

There are some conditions for reaching this level of glory in God. As noted in the scriptures, there must be an unyielding faith in God as well as expressions of praise, love, and worship of Him. The saints of old had intercessory prayer and fasted for several days until they were under the anointing. While at this stage of communicating with God, they were taken up into His glorious presence.

Several scriptures indicate His glory and the power thereof, such as **Habakkuk 3:4**, which says, *"His radiance is like the sunlight; He has rays flashing from His hand, And there is the hiding of His power."*

1 Kings 8:10-11 says, *"It happened that when the priests came from the holy place, the cloud filled the house of the LORD, so that the priests could not stand to minister because of the cloud, for the glory of the LORD filled the house of the LORD."* **Hebrew 1:3** says, *"And He is the radiance of his glory and the exact representation of his nature, and upholds all things by the word of* his power. When he had made purification of sins, he sat down at the right hand of the Majesty on high."

John 1: 14 says, *"And the Word became flesh and dwelt among us, and we saw His glory, as of the only begotten from the Father, full of grace and truth."* Glory is also referred to in **2 Peter 1:17**, *For when He received honor and glory from God the Father, such an utterance as this was made to Him by the Majestic Glory, "This is My Beloved Son with whom I am well-pleased."*

It is amazing when we think about this glory and how it has been imparted to us. It is because of our kinship and the inheritance that we receive by believing in God and accepting Jesus as our Lord and Savior. **Romans 8:17** says, *"And if children, heirs also, heirs of God and fellow heirs with Christ, if indeed we suffer with Him so that we may also be glorified with Him."* This truth nugget is brought home when Paul said in **2 Cor. 3:18**, *"But we all, with unveiled face, beholding as in a mirror the glory of the Lord, are being transformed into the same image from glory to glory, just as from the Lord, the Spirit."*

Paul discusses a passage of scripture he wrote in **1 Cor. 13:12**, (paraphrased), when we do not have a solid walk with God, we are looking through a dull and cloudy mirror. We cannot see His face or our face. However, he says in verse 18, (paraphrased), when we began to trust and truly have faith in God, the mirror becomes clear because the veil is removed from our eyes. When we look in the mirror, we no longer see a blurred figure. We see His face because He is in us and we are in Him. We are walking images of His glory.

Paul sums up the Glory of God in **Romans 8:18 (KJV)** by saying, *"For I reckon that the sufferings of this present time are not worthy to be compared with the glory which shall be revealed in us."* Paul is saying be content in your suffering because it is nothing like experiencing the glory living within us and manifested through our faith when we truly understand and began living through and for Him.

When we truly accept Jesus Christ as our Savior and the Son of a living God, we become one with the Father, the Son, and the Holy Spirit. They live in us and we live in them and our thoughts are about them. We love as they love. We take joy in all things as they do. We are slow to get angry and quick to forgive. We see only the good in every person we meet because now we can look beyond their faults and focus only on their needs. We have a burning desire to reach out to the oppressed, the persecuted, those in bondage and those locked behinds bars of insecurity, doubt, and depression.

Finally, we must be mindful that spiritual warfare should not be considered as an afterthought or a bandwagon to jump on out of popularity or a passing moment of interest. It must be taken seriously and not for granted. Everyone is not gifted to engage in spiritual warfare, especially when they do not know anything about the Holy Spirit. It is vital to use prayer for its intended purpose, which is communication with God. Prayer is not to be used as a weapon of evil intent to harm or injure an enemy. There is no place for reversing or canceling the prayers of believers.

The armor protects us from all forms of battle whether they are physical or in the mind. One should also recognize that intercession is another form of warfare that requires a closer walk with God. A true intercessor is often plagued with demonic forces that follow and torments them. Spiritual warfare and intercession are tools God has given us for protection against Satan.

OTHER FORMS OF SPIRITUAL WARFARE
Chapter 7

Intercession, declaration and proclamation are other forms of spiritual warfare that, although they require armor, does not limit the believer. These forms of warfare allow the believer to speak to demonic forces and principalities through decrees and assertions. They allow the believer to demand, rebuke and reprove processes of evil as well as the works of evildoers.

The person who enters these areas of spiritual warfare must be sure this is what he/she wants. Once this realm is crossed there is no turning back because demonic forces will attack the believer as well as family members to get to the believer. It was the belief that this was one of the primary reasons for the building of monasteries and nunneries during the early ages of Christianity, to protect the families of monks and nuns from demonic forces that followed them.   Intercession is a form of warfare where the believer stands in the gap for a friend, loved one or a child. While in this position, the believer is standing between good and evil as well as the blessings of Heaven and the principalities of Hell. This is an uncomfortable position to be in when the believer is not suited in armor nor rooted and grounded in the word of God. That is why it is important to learn certain scriptures spoken by Jesus, so you can rebuke and reprove the enemy. There are some evil forces that will not move until you call out the name of Jesus and use the exact words He used to remove that force.

When 911 occurred, many people were concerned about the souls of those who were in the twin tower and whether they were saved or whether they were snatched by Satan during this evil work. I recall going to bed that night with those thoughts on my mind and praying for the families of those who lost loved ones in the fire. I had a vision and was taken up to a place where I was in the middle of the burning tower and was in the body of a man in his office who had on khaki pants, a light blue shirt, and a dark tie. I heard the explosion and felt a burst of intense heat entering the office. The man stood up. I felt his fear and his heart beating so fast as if his chest would burst. I felt his body began to melt as the intense flames entered his office. I also felt my body being ejected from his body in time to see Jesus walk in his office and plucked his soul from his body.

Figure 40

SPIRITUAL WARFARE

Then I saw Him walk through every floor in the towers at the same time collecting souls. They were blue flashes of light like diamonds that were attracted to Him like magnets. He caught them and gathered them all in the palm of his hands. I looked for scriptures as proof of what I saw and found **Malachi 3:17** which says, *"And they shall be mine, says the LORD of hosts, in that day when I make up my jewels; and I will spare them, as a man spares his own son that serves him."*

Another form of spiritual warfare is declaration where we say, "I declare, decree or command," Satan and the forces of evil to loose and remove a stronghold from a person. I received a call one night from a young man wanting prayer. He said his life was full of darkness, anger, and hatred. He could not sleep or rest. He was begging for relief from the torment and hellfire he was encountering. I began praying for him over the phone. I felt a surge of power and authority take charge of my voice and my body as my prayer became intense and fiery. When I finished praying, I gave him instructions about what to do when fear and darkness came upon him again. I went to bed that night feeling empowered and full of the Spirit of God.

When my head hit my pillow, I saw a demon enter my room. He had dreadlocks on his head and his entire body was black and chalky like charcoal. He figured that since I had not engaged in any intimate relationships since my husband's death 14 years ago, I was starved for affection. He tried to enter my bed. I was determined that he would not touch me. I rebuked him and commanded him to get out of my room, and that I was in Jesus and He was in me. To look at me was to look at Jesus. The face broke up into tiny little particles that quickly vanished in the air. Demonic forces recognize the name of Jesus. His body began to break up in small fragments and vanished.

Figure 41

I went back to sleep but was awakened from my sleep by a giant form lurking over me. My heart began to pound, but I quickly remembered who I was in Christ. I sat up in my bed and said, "I don't fear you. I know who you are. It won't work now go back to the pit of hell." However, this form did not move as the first demon did. I knew at once that this form was the devil himself, coming to complete what the demon couldn't do. I jumped out of my bed and got my anointing oil. I anointed my head with oil and anointed my entire room.

The Holy Spirit told me to repeat verses from **Psalm 23**, *"He anointed my head with oil, my cup runs over. Surely, goodness and mercy shall follow me all the days of my life and I shall dwell in the house of the Lord forever."* The dark shadow began to recede. I went to sleep and slept in peace.

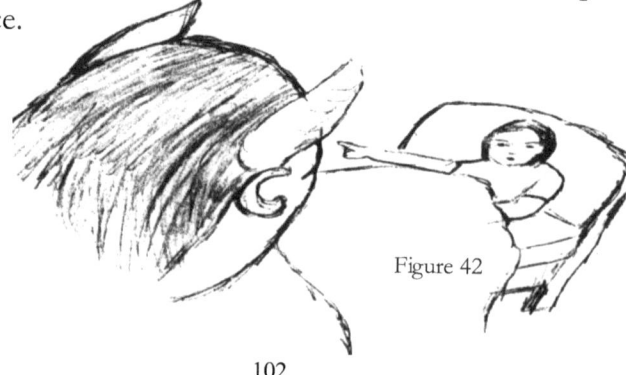

Figure 42

It is important to remember that we can command demons, demonic forces and workers of evil to leave us alone and banish them back to outer darkness, but we do not have the authority to banish Satan from the earth. We do have the authority to rebuke and reprove him, but we cannot cast him into outer darkness.

James 4:7 says, *"Resist the devil and he will flee from you."* Notice, it does not say to banish nor take authority over him. It only says to resist him and he will flee. Since we are in Christ and He is in us, demons will see Christ in us. When we operate with the authority of Christ that lives in us, we can command demons and demonic forces to leave us.

This same authority keeps Satan a certain distance from us. Satan uses demons, evildoers, and demonic forces to carry out his work upon us through lies, deception and evil deeds. He only comes after us when our resistance is too strong for demons. The only person to banish Satan will be the angel spoken of in **Revelation 20: 1-3,** who will lock him up in a bottomless pit for a thousand years.

I have discovered that as a person grows older, they began to see things that appear to be abnormal to others, but normal to them. These people are often called crazy or possessed with an evil spirit, but the closer these individuals reach a certain age, they began to see, hear and experience unusual sightings of strange objects and people. I have often heard people in their seventies and beyond speak of such things.

My prayer partner often spoke of demons that would come in her house to torment her. They would rearrange her clothes and remove her valuables. Sometimes, she would hear them at work while I was visiting her. She eventually left her bedroom and began sleeping on her couch. We engaged in warfare on a regular basis to drive these forces from her home. We spoke certain things into being and life over her situations until these forces left her home.

I have often seen spirits walking through my house. One time I saw a little boy dressed in a white robe with a white band around his waist. His hair was cut as if a bowl had been placed over his head. He had an old candle holder and lit candle in one hand and a roll of paper in the other hand. The entire image was like a projected image that appeared at my bedroom door. The image faded out and was quickly gone.

My sisters often talk about people walking through their homes from the past. They were freighted at first, but these visitors have now become a routine part of their lives. Mary told me about a young girl in pigtails that was in her house after a storm. She said the little girl looked up at her and vanished. My sister, Pearl, sees a bright light at the foot of her bed and often experiences someone sitting on her bed when death is approaching the family. I often hear a phone ringing late in the night, only to awaken and find no one has called. Then, the following morning I learn that someone in the family has died. I heard a phone ringing when my oldest sister passed, and my doorbell rang once a few minutes after her passing, but no one was there.

As I was growing stronger in my body after the initial stroke, many former members of my church came and asked me if I would ever pastor again. I wrestled with the desire to go back but was reluctant to discuss it openly with anyone. Then, one afternoon, I had a vision that I was looking for Rev. Wright to ask him about my hidden desire to pastor again.

I found him at the old wooden church that had been destroyed several decades ago. He was talking to other pastors of the church who served before after him. I turned the lights on in the front foyer and the back of the church. I did not speak to him, but I felt his presence and he knew that I was there. When it became obvious, that I would not speak to him, I decided to turn the lights off. I reached up and flipped the switch, but, the lights did not go off. They continued to burn.

I went to the foyer to turn the light off and they would not go out either. The old sexton came because he saw the lights from the road. I recognized him as the old janitor who kept the church and the church grounds clean. I also recall how he kept the baptismal pool, which was located outside the church, clear of leaves and fallen debris.

We went to the fuse box and he removed the fuses, but the lights still did not go out. I got in my car to leave and as I was driving out the front yard, I looked back and saw that Rev. Wright's office door was open. The room was empty, but the lights were still burning. I did not know immediately what these lights represented, but now I know exactly what they meant and why they were burning so bright.

Figure 43

Although I never spoke with my pastor, he left a message without saying a word. He was letting me know that the light burning inside of me will never go out. I will never be able to turn it off and no one else can turn it off either. Since the light is burning inside of me I know that I must go and do as God commands. I know what my mission is. I have fought it for a long time. I used the ministry as a shield, thinking my ministry would fulfill the call, but now the call was greater than the mission.

The more I learned about the Holy Spirit, I realized when people who are no longer with us are sent to us in dreams, it is a way God prevents danger and evildoers from destroying us. He knows that if He comes to us, as He is, we would be so scared that we would probably die of a heart attack or a stroke. When we look at Moses and see how his appearance changed every time he came before God, we know that no one can look upon Him and remain the same. God must use someone we trust, a parent, a mentor or a loved one to communicate with us. Spiritual warfare is an area where loved ones from our past are often used as messengers and angels to warn us of danger and help us fight our battles. **Psalm 91:11-12** says *"He shall give His angels charge over us."* Sometimes God sends Jesus as an angel or He comes Himself to help us survive in a world where Satan has been given charge over our lives.

We must wrestle with principalities, rulers of darkness and spiritual wickedness in high places as we live on earth. However, knowing that there is someone who will fight our battles for us, give us peace, security, and strength to receive the victory is comforting. When we carry a song and a verse in our heart, we soon realize that weeping may endure for a night, but joy comes in the morning.

The following sketches are visions that I have seen. I do not know when they will take place I only know that these are warnings of things to come:

The figure seen below is of a national leader whose mouth will be closed by an angel. This world leader is often looking for evidence of events that have taken place or have been stated that will come to pass. The angel will place both hands over this person's mouth and slowly lay him back to rest. I searched the scriptures for a reference to this vision and was taken to **Luke**

1:18-25 where an angel told Zechariah about a child he would have in his old age. Zechariah demanded proof from the angel. The angel told Zechariah that because of his unbelief, his mouth would be closed for several months until the child was born. The same thing will happen to this world leader. So often God will reduce us to a small fragment to let us know who is truly in charge of what takes place on the world's stage.

Figure 44

Another vision is of a large plane that stretches several miles in width and length. This plane was seen from 35 miles away in a neighboring county as I was driving home from taking my son to work. I was amazed by the size of the plane and thought others could see this massive airplane hovering in the sky, above what appeared to be a hospital. I was expecting to see cars parked on the side of the road and people looking up into the sky, but all the cars were still moving on the highway. Evidently, I was the only person to see this plane. This open vision played in my mind for several days. The plane was so close that I could see the fans inside the engines of the plane. I could also see inside the cockpit, but could not see a pilot or any passengers aboard. The beam from the bottom of the plane appeared to stretch out over several miles.

Figure 45

I searched the Scriptures for an account of this vision and I was taken to the book of **Zechariah 5:1-2** which says, *"Then I lifted up my eyes again and looked, and behold, there was a flying scroll. And He said to me, 'What do you see?' And I answered, 'I see a flying scroll; its length is twenty cubits and its width ten cubits"* I'm reminded of another verse from **1 Thess. 4:17** which says, *"Then, we which are alive and remain shall be caught up together with them in the clouds, to meet the Lord in the air: and so, shall we ever be with the Lord."*

Another future vision I had concerns the fall of religious leaders, false doctrines and a massive fall-away from the church. The flood water, in figure 46 below, represents the great number of people who will be affected by this fall. The greatest damage will be done to people who are controlled by drug demons, sex demons, and stronghold demons.

These people will no longer look to church leaders to deliver them from these demonic forces. There will be a great increase in the number of false prophets and teachers who claim to have divine powers to release them from these strongholds. There are several scriptures which support this vision.

Figure 46

This vision is also an indication of future floods and torrential rainfall that will destroy houses, people, land, and cities throughout the world. A scripture to validate this vision is the flood found in the Old Testament where the earth and its inhabitants were destroyed by water.

Another future vision is the onset of strange air vehicles which will be seen in the sky near the edges of the sea. These aircrafts are triangular and, have three propellers at the end of each point. These propellers allow the craft to move up and down and hover closer to the ground or any stationary object. These crafts also have a large space capacity and can carry many individuals or material.

There are other future visions that The Holy Spirit has revealed to me about several events that are coming to pass. I have learned to pray when I feel danger approaching. I have also learned that when we get closer to God, He will show us all things, past, present, and future. **1 Corinthians 2:1**.

Recently I had three visitors who appeared at the foot of my bed. One was a policeman who reached out to me around 3:00 am. I started rebuking what he was experiencing and started praying for him and the situation he was in. I awakened to the news of the shooting in Las Vegas and learned that a policeman lost his life in the shooting.

The next night I was awakened by a young girl standing at my bedside holding a toddler. I began praying for her and her child. I later learned that a young girl I had met some months ago was in an accident with her toddler. They both survived the terrible wreck that totaled her car.

I am going to bed tonight, eagerly waiting to see what the Holy Spirit will reveal to me in the spirit realm, so I can defeat Satan's plan by rebuking and praying for his next victims. I am ready to go to war for whoever shows up on the opposite side, or the foot of my bed. I thank God that I know what to do for the wandering spirits.

I thank God, He has restored my body and has given me the faith and security I had as a child. I have a limp in my left leg because of the strokes I endured five years ago. I have asked God to remove it, but if He doesn't, I am at peace. I am reminded of Paul when he prayed to God to remove the thorn from his side, God replied, "My grace is sufficient for you."

APPENDIX

Warfare Scriptures

The following scriptures are a compilation of verses that can be used in spiritual warfare:

1. 2 Chron. 20:15
2. Eph. 6:11-17
3. Isaiah 54:17
4. Luke 10:19
5. Romans 8:37
6. 2 Thess. 3:3
7. Matt. 18: 18-19
8. 1 Cor. 10:13
9. Deut. 28:7
10. 1 Tim. 6:12
11. Rev. 12:11
12. Deut. 3:22
13. Psalm 24:5
14. Joshua 1:19
15. 2 Cor. 10:4
16. Col. 2:15
17. Deut. 20:1
18. Isaiah 41:10
19. Phil. 4:13
20. 1 Peter 5: 8-9
21. Psalm 27:1
22. Col. 3:12-15
23. 1 Peter 5:7
24. Gal. 5:22-23
25. Matt. 5:6
26. 1 John 3:8
27. Mark 23:6
28. John 8:44
29. John 4:24
30. 2 Cor. 2:11
31. 1 John 5:14
32. Eph. 6:18
33. John 17:15
34. James 5:13
35. Mark 11:24
36. Matt. 5:44
37. Proverbs 15:8
38. Romans 8:26
39. Phil. 4:6
40. 1Thess. 5:17

11 Scriptures on Healing, taken from the NIV Bible

1. **James 5:14** *If there is among you sick? Let them call the elders of the church to pray over them and anoint them with oil in the name of the Lord*
2. **Psalm 147:3** *He Heals the broken-hearted and binds up their wounds.*

3. **Isaiah 53:5** *But He was pierced for our transgressions, He was crushed for our iniquities; the punishment that brought us peace was on Him, and by His wounds we are healed.*
4. **Jeremiah 30:17** *For I will restore health to you and your wounds I will heal, declares the Lord.*
5. **Luke 10:9** *Heal the sick and say to them, the Kingdom of God has come to you.*
6. **Acts 4:30** *While (I) you stretch out (my) your hand to heal, signs and wonders are performed through the name of your Holy Servant, Jesus.*
7. **James 5:16** *Confess your sins to one another and pray for one another that you may be healed. The effectual fervent prayers of a righteous man avail much.*
8. **Mark 5:34** *Jesus said unto her, "Daughter, your faith has healed you, go in peace and be free of your suffering.*
9. **Jeremiah 33:6** *Behold I will bring them health and healing and I will heal them and reveal to them an abundance of prosperity and security.*
10. **Psalm 41:4** *I said, "O Lord, be gracious to me; heal me, for I have sinned against you."*
11. **Psalm 41:3** *The Lord will sustain him upon his sickbed: In his illness, you restore him to health.*

These verses are effective when your name or the sick person's name is used when read.

References

Bibles Search for Scriptures
1. KJV: King James Version
2. NKJV: New King James Version
3. NIV: New International Version
4. ESV: English Standard Version
5. RSV: Revised Standard Version
6. ESB: English Standard Bible

Religious Texts

1. Brown, F. Driver, S. & C Briggs, 2010, The Brown, Driver and Briggs Hebrew and English Lexicon, Peabody: Mass, Hendrickson Publishers
2. Webster's Unabridged Dictionary, 1913
3. Wilkerson, D. 1999, The Effects of seeing the Glory of God.
   http://www.tscpulpitseries.org/English/1990s/ts990621.html

ABOUT THE AUTHOR

Reverend Frances W. Cox was the seventh child born to her parents in Anderson, SC. Her parents were adamant about making certain their children were religiously trained. Fran, affectionately called by some friends and family, was educated in the public schools in her county and completed higher degrees in the sciences. She aspired to become a medical doctor, but decided to become a physics and chemistry teacher instead.

Cox also became an ordained and licensed minister while holding a job as a teacher.

She continued her Christian education at Liberty Theological Seminary in Lynchburg, Virginia and received a divinity degree to assist her while pastoring a church full time.

There was always a calling on Cox's life and it was proven many times over in dreams and visions as a child. Fran's mother was very protective of her because a fetus was discovered while she was prepping for surgery to remove tumors from her reproductive system. That was probably the mother-daughter link that made them almost inseparable. They had an incredible closeness.

Because of the many obstacles and challenges wrought by the forces of evil to bring demise to Frances' spirit, soul and body, she decided to pen this book to describe her experiences and the forces in the world that are constantly at odds with each other. As an illustrator, Frances Cox shows how these forces came and were defeated. This book shows how the reader may use these examples and Scriptures inserted in the appendix to overcome impossibilities in their lives. Cox is a published author of the book entitled, **The Woman's Daily Meditations in Psalms** published 2015 by West Bow Press.

www.ingramcontent.com/pod-product-compliance
Lightning Source LLC
Chambersburg PA
CBHW042053290426
44110CB00006B/167